Residential Care Services for the Elderly: Business Guide for Home-Based Eldercare

Residential Care Services for the Elderly: Business Guide for Home-Based Eldercare

Doris K. Williams

Routledge
Taylor & Francis Group

LONDON AND NEW YORK

First published by
The Haworth Press, Inc.
10 Alice Street
Binghamton, N Y 13904-1580

This edition published 2011 by Routledge

Routledge
Taylor & Francis Group
711 Third Avenue
New York, NY 10017

Routledge
Taylor & Francis Group
2 Park Square
Milton Park, Abingdon
Oxon OX14 4RN

Residential Care Services for the Elderly: Business Guide for Home-Based Eldercare has also been published as the *Journal of Housing for the Elderly*, Volume 8, Number 2 1991.

The Haworth Press, Inc. 10 Alice Street, Binghamton, NY 13904-1580
EUROSPAN/Haworth, 3 Henrietta Street, London WC2E 8LU England
ASTAM/Haworth, 162-168 Parramatta Road, Stanmore, Sydney, N.S.W. 2048 Australia

Library of Congress Cataloging-in-Publication Data

Residential care services for the elderly: business guide for home-based eldercare / Doris K. Williams.
    p. cm.
    "Has also been published as the Journal of housing for the elderly, volume 8, number 2, 1991"—T.p. verso.
    ISBN 1-56024-152-7 (acid free paper)   ISBN 0-7890-0066-0 (acid free paper)
    1. Aged—Institutional care—United States—Handbooks, manuals, etc. 2. Group homes—United States—Handbooks, manuals, etc. 3. Caregivers—United States—Handbooks, manuals, etc. 4. Home-based businesses—United States—Handbooks, manuals, etc. I. Williams, Doris K.
HV1465.R47 1991
362.6'3—dc20   91-34626
                                                    CIP

Dedication

This publication is dedicated to my mother:

Ina G. Honaker Keaton
Hinton, West Virginia

Regardless of her severe pain and poor physical health prior to her death in November 1989, her spirit, sense of humor, and personal fortitude served as a model for those of us who were younger and active in designing programs for the elderly. One of my personal and professional goals is to replicate her philosophy of life which is based on "service to others."

ABOUT THE AUTHOR

Doris K. Williams, PhD, is Professor of Human Resource Development and Specialist in Gerontology at the School of Home Economics of the University of Idaho in Moscow. She has devoted the last five years to research and extension gerontology, one result of this dedication being *Shelter Care Services for the Rural Elderly: A Home-Based Business Handbook*. This book has also been developed into an education program designed for delivery through the USDA Cooperative Extension System. Dr. William has written for the *Adult Residential Care Journal, The Journal of Consumer Studies and Home Economics*, and *The Idaho Economy*. She received her PhD in Family and Child Development from The Ohio State University in Columbus and her Master's in Management/Family from Ohio University in Athens. Dr. Williams is a member of the American Home Economics Association, the National Council of Family Relations, the American Society on Aging, and the Association for Women in Development.

Residential Care Services for the Elderly: Business Guide for Home-Based Eldercare

CONTENTS

Foreword

With the escalating proportion of the United States population over age sixty-five, attention is focusing on the increasing demand for care services for the elderly. A variety of care options are becoming available including providing care for elderly individuals in residential homes. This book provides information to assist individuals who are contemplating establishing a for-profit home based business to provide residential care services for elderly people. It addresses an individual's interests and abilities, potential clients' needs and motivations, and describes issues and procedures involved in residential care. The presentation of the material is unique in that it provides practical information on residential care homes from the perspective of both the potential business owner and the needs of the potential client. It is important to consider the human element in addition to the business orientation.

The information is divided into seven major sections. The first four sections provide vital information on the numerous aspects of operating a care facility in a residence, including the degree of need for shelter care homes, steps involved in implementing a facility, facility management, and financial aspects. The last three sections provide supporting information, resources, summarize the text content and draw conclusions.

The background section (Chapter 1) provides a profile of older persons including conditions which affect a family's ability to provide care for an aging family member. It describes the increasing need for shelter care in light of the fact that many elderly who are placed in nursing homes could be cared for in the familial atmosphere of a residential care setting with the advantage of expanded opportunities to meet clients' needs for socialization and frequent interpersonal contacts.

In Chapter 2 general information about implementation is presented. This information includes descriptions of the types of care services, information on the procedures involved to get a facility licensed, a description of private and governmental funding sources, and a discussion of emotional and financial factors to be considered when contemplating operating a facility.

Chapter 3 focuses on facility management, beginning with assessment of the feasibility of an individual starting a care facility home-based business. In this section, self-assessment questions are provided to help determine if a person has the personal characteristics associated with successfully providing care and to determine the adaptability of a home to a care facility. This section also highlights items associated with success as a business entrepreneur. Suggestions for effective facility management include developing an organizational chart, determining facility policies (such as taking clients for a two week trial period), choosing a client contract format, establishing a fee schedule, staffing, providing food service, conforming to regulations, meeting client needs and recruiting clients.

In Chapter 4 suggestions are made for developing a financial plan. These suggestions include preparation of an income statement, balance sheet, cash flow statement and a statement of projected profits. Risks associated with operating a care facility are portrayed and risk management through insurance coverage is presented. Sources of tax expertise for this type of business are presented.

The next section (Chapter 5) provides supplementary information of particular interest because it includes a portrayal of the changing demographics of the population in relation to a care facility business. This material encompasses a description of rural and urban environments that support growth in residential care homes. The establishment of home based care businesses may help to revitalize communities affected by a declining economy. Various parts of the country are experiencing shifts in the population of older people, and the resulting demand for care services. The particular needs of the frail elderly are described. Studies are mentioned that point out the advantages to both the business person and the elderly client and their family of a residential care home as an alternative to a nursing home. The income opportunities associated with greater demand for residential care are proffered.

Chapter 6 encourages networking and seeking a wide range of available resources when determining the feasibility of opening a residential care facility. These resources provide valuable insight in regard to the myriad of choices to be considered when making the decision to initiate operation of a residential care facility in one's home. A variety of case situations provide a range of viewpoints of residential care home owners, as they explain their reasons for operating their homes and describe how they feel about their business and their clients.

This "how to" handbook can be used by health care professionals, as a text in courses focusing on establishing a small home-based business, and by social service agencies who are considering alternatives for their elderly clients. In summary (Chapter 7) a residential care home can benefit both the provider and the resident by providing income while offering a long term care option that enables elderly to have a higher quality of life.

Virginia W. Junk, PhD
Assistant Professor
Family and Consumer Studies
University of Idaho
Moscow, Idaho

Acknowledgements

The author gratefully acknowledges the constructive reviews of both the preliminary proposal and this final manuscript by Dr. Marjory Woodburn, Professor, Foods and Nutrition, Oregon State University; Dr. Clara Pratt, Director, Program on Gerontology and Professor, Human Development and Family Studies, Oregon State University; Dr. Victor A. Christopherson, Professor, School of Family and Consumer Resources, University of Arizona; Dr. Glenn R. Hawkes, Professor, Department of Applied Behavioral Sciences, University of California; Dr. Barbara Gunn, Gerontology Specialist, University of Nevada; and Dr. Vicki Schmall, Extension Specialist in Gerontology, Oregon State University.

Special appreciation is also expressed to Dr. Russ Youmans, Director of the Western Rural Development Center which funded the project.

The following shelter home operators provided important forms of subjective insight and practical suggestions:

Belinda and Pat Kelly;
Mary and Clifford Blanck;
Carolyn and Dale Hawk;
Helen Derr.

Other consultants who provided valuable assistance are:

Dr. William H. Parks, Professor of Finance, Department of Business, University of Idaho;
Judy Helms, AOA Ombudsman, Idaho Falls;
Cyndee McDanial, Administrative Assistant, Home Call of Oregon;
Eleanor Long, Editor;
Debbie Rumford, Computer Technician.

Lastly, Offices of Health and Welfare of the states of Idaho, Oregon, and Washington offered technical information and sample standards.

BOX 1

EARLY 1970'S

In the early 1970's, the land-grant institutions established four regional rural development centers. These regional centers were started to initiate and support research in conjunction with State Agricultural Experiment Stations. The extension responsibility was quickly added to bring research and extension together for regional rural development work. The Centers promote community education programs and training of faculty to deliver research based programs to rural communities.

Note: These Centers continue to coordinate and encourage research and extension work on topics important to agriculture and community viability. They have been able to respond quickly to emerging concerns, such as the alternatives available to rural communities and families confronted by dramatic ecomonic changes. This handbook is one example.

Purpose

This handbook is designed to help you determine the feasibility of starting a small home business to provide residential home services — sometimes referred to as Residential Care Homes or Adult Foster Care Homes — for one or more elderly persons.

Chapters 1 and 2 provide rationale and information concerning "how" to determine if a small shelter home business would be appropriate for you; if so, Chapter 1 provides details on how to start and maintain your business. Chapter 5 explains "why" starting small rural shelter home businesses is important.

As an educational aid, the handbook will serve as a basis for your decision making while helping you assess your need for further training or technical assistance. Opportunities for networking among state licensing/standards agencies, funding agencies, as well as elder care organizations and advocacy groups such as Area Offices on Aging (AOA) will also be described.

Trends underscore a growing need for long-term care alternatives and for welfare and local planning in non-metropolitan areas where older people are disproportionately concentrated. Because the aim of this handbook is to assist individuals in assessing their interests in and abilities to establish profit-making residential care home businesses, the strategy for generating this income will focus on private funds or a combination of sources of funds to equal a legitimate level of profit.

Limitations

There are numerous types of services that are needed and can be designed to service the elderly. While these will be mentioned in this handbook, the major emphasis here is on residential homes — or similar intermediate care environments sometimes called Adult Foster Care Homes. The handbook is written in a generalized format — meaning that the concepts are not specific to any one state but can be used to give direction, promote ideas, and serve as guidance tools. It's important to understand that each state will have specific standards and requirements, and, therefore, state agencies should be contacted accordingly.

The author hereby submits a statment disavowing any claim brought as a result of information contained in this handbook.

Chapter 1

Background:
Defining the Need
for Residential Care Homes

The condition of a large elderly population is new. This is the first time in world history that such a large proportion of the population is 65 years of age and over. The average life span in ancient Greece was only 18, but by 1600 in the U.S. it was 33; in 1900 it was 47; in 1970 it was about 70, and a child born in 1987 can expect to live to be 74.9. With this "new" elderly population, there has been an emerging social awareness of the impact of senior citizens on society as it functions (see Box 2).[1]

The concerns of the elderly have become concerns of the nation. The aging of the American population is both a success story today and a challenge for the future. Older people, who are rapidly growing in number and in proportion to the total population, are living proof of progress this nation has made in health care including long-term care, nutrition, housing, and other critical human service areas (Rogers, 1986). Table 1 clearly shows how rapidly the numbers of elderly are increasing.

In 1987 there were 17.7 million older women and 12.1 million older men, or a sex ratio of 146 women for every 100 men. The sex ratio increased with age, ranging from 120 for the 65-69 group or a high of 256 for persons 85 and older. Since 1900, the percentage of Americans 65 + has tripled (4.1% in 1900 to 12.3% in 1987), and the number increased over nine times (from 3.1 million to 29.8 million).

The older population itself is getting older. In 1987 the 65-74 age group (17.7 million) was eight times larger than in 1900, but the 75-

Box 2

GROWTH AND NEED TO PLAN

By 2010 there will come a remarkable surge in the numbers of older persons as the post-war baby boom matures. In less than 30 years, an aging society will be upon us, whether we have prepared for it or not.

The very old, while making up only about 9 % of the older population in 1980, will account for almost one-fourth of the projected growth in the older population over the next 20 years. If we anticipate and plan for this momentous social event now, individuals and families can still adjust their own expectations and plans for the future.

2

TABLE 1

NUMBER OF PERSONS 65+ IN U.S.
1900 TO 2030

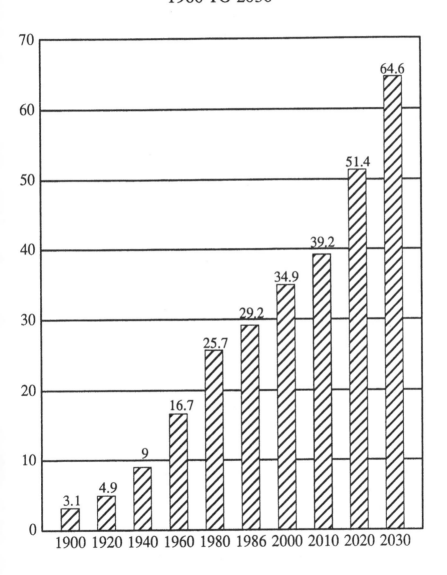

84 group (9.3 million) was 12 times larger and the 85 + group (2.9 million) was 23 times larger. The older population is expected to continue to grow in the future (see Tables 1 and 2). By the year 2030 the "over 85" group, which is the most vulnerable to poor health and therefore has the greatest need for long-term care facilities, will almost triple (AARP, 1988).

Though the family is the primary caregiver for the elderly, its structure is changing and this will influence caregiving in the future (Research & News Update, 1988).[2]

Some examples of these changes are the increasing divorce rate, which may decrease the availability of a spouse as a caregiver; the decreasing size of the American family, which leaves fewer children available to support parents; and the increased participation by women in the labor force, which decreases the amount of informal care available in the home. In addition, the children of today's elderly are themselves approaching their retirement years and may be less physically and financially able to assist older parents.

In view of this rapidly emerging social situation, more facets of our society are, for the first time, considering this age group: its characteristics, problems, assets, liabilities and impact on the entire society. Regardless of causes, there is a serious need for planning and facilitating long-term care environments.[3]

NEED FOR RESIDENTIAL CARE HOMES

According to Sirocco (1988), the *Inventory of Long-Term Care Places* indicated that, of all types of long-term care facilities of three beds or more, the for-profit residential homes with 20 beds or less were smallest in number. The West had smaller sized units, but Sirocco hypothesized that this was because the population in this region is more dispersed. Persons in residential facilities, as compared with nursing homes, tended to be younger. In addition, residential facilities displayed much more variation by ownership than did nursing homes.[4]

One Advance Data Survey (Sirocco, 1987), indicated that the greatest number (4,578) of residential homes has 3-9 beds, the second greatest number (2,626) has 10-24 beds and the third (1,074) has 50-74 beds. By far they are profit-making businesses (as com-

TABLE 2

U.S. Residents, 65 Years and Older, 1960 - 2030*

	AGE 65-74	AGE 75-84	AGE 85 +
1960	10,997 (6.1%)	4,633 (2.6%)	929 (.5%)
1970	12,443 (6.1%)	6,122 (3.0%)	1,408 (.7%)
1980	15,578 (6.9%)	7,727 (3.4%)	2,240 (1.%)

TABLE 2 (continued)

	AGE 65-74	AGE 75-84	AGE 85 +
2000	17,436 (6.7%)	10,630 (4.1%)	3,756 (1.4%)
2030	31,853 (10.6%)	17,489 (5.8%)	5,681 (1.9%)

* Numbers in 1000s

pared with government or non-profit) and the greatest percent (11.6) were in the West with 8.4 percent in the Midwest.

Another study showing trends which verify the need for long-term care services is the *1987 National Hospital Discharge Survey* (1988). This study found that hospital discharge rate has continued a decline that began in 1983. The 1987 rate was 138 discharges per 1000 civilian population, a 17 percent decrease in 4 years. A decade ago the average length of stay was 7.6 days and in 1987 it was 6.4 days. This decline could indicate the need for intermediate care facilities, such as that offered by a residential home environment.[5]

Residential care, shelter homes or adult foster homes are often the first choice for individuals in need of long-term care. Making a decision to seek a residential home environment and selecting a home can be a difficult, often an emotional process for both the older individual and the family. The transition from the elderly's life at home to his or her life in a group living situation can be challenging for all involved. Such change requires time to make adjustments. While there are a number of problems and concerns in regard to this transition, there are also many benefits to be gained (AARP, 1987).[6]

Residential homes provide families the capacity for creating new income-producing services that will meet the needs of a community in these changing times. Should families and communities create residential care, they will not only provide a much needed service for the elderly at a lower cost than institutional care, but they also will generate new jobs and income to be expended in the community (Price, 1982).

PROFILE OF THE OLDER PERSON

The elderly have a range of social and medical needs arising from a variety of life situations — especially isolated living arrangements and declining health (Halpert and Isbell, 1988).[7]

Some elderly persons follow a monotonous routine offering little of the mental and physical stimulation necessary for their continued development and well-being. In a sheltered environment, they can share their feelings and gain support from their peers. Even the loss of brain function can be slowed by stimulation. And, ongoing interpersonal contacts are easier to provide in a residential care program than in the traditional in-home service programs (Home Call & Oregon, 1987).

Studies suggest that up to one-third of the elderly in nursing homes are unnecessarily confined. Contrary to the stereotype, most elderly persons are relatively healthy and, even with chronic illness, are not as limited as frequently assumed. Although many elderly can no longer manage such everyday chores as preparing meals, taking medication, shopping, walking, toileting, or feeding, they do not need 24-hour nursing-care supervision, but rather assistance and socialization. Residential homes are ideally designed to provide this type of care. They might also prevent premature hospitalization.[8]

The problem is even more severe for the rural elderly, who are the most likely to have chronic health conditions that limit activities and to require health care assistance, even though it is less available to them than to their healthier metropolitan peers.

As the U.S. population shifts, more and more Americans will find themselves confronted with an aging parent requiring care. Help will come not from bigger and better nursing homes, but from developing ways to support a family caring system. Increasingly, residential homes are desired options for long-term care (Isabell and Halpert, 1986). Because residential home care is growing in popularity, program development, research, and public policies will need to be addressed continuously. Standards for quality programs are being refined, and communication networks and advocacy organizations for residential home operators are rapidly being organized.[9]

The quality of life for the frail elderly has greatly contributed to the need for this handbook. Residential homes will enable the elderly to remain in their resident communities, and this, in turn, will add to the stability and vitality of rural areas (MacLeon, 1987).

Chapter 2

General Information
Concerning Implementation

TYPES OF SERVICES

Most of us know someone who is giving continuous care to a person who is infirmed, impaired or needing help with one or more daily activities. Most of this type of care is given at home by family members, most frequently spouses and adult children. For many, this demand imposes a difficult situation, and, with time, families may need to look for or consider alternative types of assistance. Some of these alternative are outlined in Box 3.

The patient's functional abilities, need for service, and financial resources will determine the appropriateness of each adult care program choice, assuming there is one or more available. The emergence of these types of programs is relatively new, and there are advantages and disadvantages to each. Segal and Moyles (1988) agree with this author on the general function of residential homes but have also developed a topology which could be a useful descriptive model to service more specific groups (e.g., mentally ill, handicapped, etc.).

STANDARDS AND LICENSING

Residential care homes are considered to be a "social" care model in contrast to the "medical" model of nursing home services. Standards for each differ greatly.

Standards for residential homes — or adult foster care homes — are much less complex. Individuals who can benefit from residential

BOX 3

DEFINITIONS: TYPES OF SERVICES

Home health care covers a wide variety of services to help maintain the older person at home. Sometimes this will be under a doctor's supervision. It can include medical services provided by trained professionals, such as nurses or physical therapists, or personal care services, such as assistance with grooming or dressing, provided by homemaker-home health aides. Home health care services may be offered by area agencies on aging, visiting nurse associations, hospitals, and many profit or non-profit organizations.

Adult day care is a program attended on a daily basis: the patient may attend a center from three to seven hours a day, five days a week or two or three days a week. Often a midday meal is provided. The program offers families relief in the assurance that their loved ones are receiving care from trained sources during the hours when no one can be at home. Adult day care services range from socialization to health related care. Some adult day care centers will not accept Alzheimer's patients. Others may accept Alzheimer's patients in the early stages of the disease. However, there are some day care centers that have been established especially for patients with Alzheimer's disease and related disorders.

Residential Home or Adult Foster Care service is a family setting where the elderly person is treated like an extended family member. Bedrooms may be shared, and meals are served in a family setting. This residential care can be provided by a family or by another elderly person who still maintains his or her home. The level of service in this "social model" is most suitable for those who can no longer remain in their own homes but do not need the medical services of nursing homes. Many state standards for residential homes require that clients be ambulatory.

Custodial nursing home care is for people who primarily require assistance with personal care, such as bathing, dressing, and eating.

Intermediate nursing home care is for people who don't require skilled care but who typically do need some nursing assistance and supervision.

Skilled nursing facility is the type of service for people who need 24-hour-a-day care and supervision by a registered nurse. Physicians direct these environments and are available in cases of emergency.

care situations for the most part need supervision and assistance but not continuous medical attention. Though standards may vary somewhat from state to state, all attempts have been made to ensure legally a safe and healthy homelike environment.

Because of the growth in need and popularity of residential care homes, many states are currently updating licensing standards and procedures. Exact or current sets of standards and licensing procedures can be obtained from respective state offices on Welfare or Human Services. Sample topics that will likely be addressed are presented in Box 4.

Having state licensing and certification ensures standardization of some quality measures in the care process, and, standards can be monitored. However, published standards are usually minimal and several aspects of residential or foster care responsibilities go beyond strict adherence to printed standards.

SINCE STATE STANDARDS VARY, YOU WILL NEED TO CHECK WITH THE RESPECTIVE HUMAN SERVICES OR PUBLIC WELFARE OFFICES TO OBTAIN COPIES THAT APPLY TO YOUR STATE.

EFFECTIVENESS OF STANDARDS

An annual assessment is conducted by the respective state licensing or certification agency. You, the operator of a residential home, can benefit greatly from annual assessment by state licensing personnel. Their reports should be, and often are, shared with State Office of Aging ombudsmen. Some states go so far as to have a memorandum of agreement wherein assessment reports are shared.

It is to your benefit to participate in the annual assessment process and to communicate with both the licensing personnel and ombudsman representative. The ombudsman will be your friend and advocate. He or she can help you locate resources and follow-up with other needs.

Beyond the standards, the ombudsman will also be able to judge the quality of the services delivered through your business. He or she will likely talk to the elderly residents, asking them whether or not they've had visitors, how clients like the home, whether or not the food is cooked the way they like it, whether a variety of types of foods are available, etc. The ombudsman will also ask whether the clients have choices, have family members or friends who visit, what specific things they like or dislike about the residential home, and whether they are paid attention to and really cared about. Questions might also include: Do they get to keep some of their own belongings in their rooms? Do they get to go out of doors? Are there animals to pet? Are there ever children around for them to interact with? Are they ever hugged or given affection?

These respective criteria may be useful in self-assessment and also be the type used by officials in the initial annual licensing review which is conducted by the respective state agency responsible for licensing or certification (e.g., State Department of Public Welfare or Health and Human Services). This licensing review process will likely determine your initial and subsequent licensing or certification status. Generalized procedures include the following:

1. First, the applicant informs the Bureau of Facility Standards of his or her intentions; the office will send a standard informational packet, including several necessary documents, to the applicant.
2. With the completed forms and a request for a building evaluation returned to the Bureau of Facility Standards, the prospective residential home owner will need to include a processing fee, typically $100.00.
3. Upon the initial visit, the inspector will itemize the building changes to be made; after the alterations are complete, the applicant will request another visit.
4. When the building and grounds are approved, the applicant receives a temporary license, good usually for six months.
5. During this probation period, a survey team visits the facility to see that the operation is in compliance with all regulations. Usually during these visits, a large number of deficient areas are identified.
6. Before the full license is granted, the applicant must assure the respective public office of his or her willingness and ability to meet the regulations on a continuing basis.

BOX 4

SAMPLE TOPICS IN RESIDENTIAL CARE STANDARDS

Authority

Adult family homes

Definitions

Application for license investigation

Licensing of state employees

General qualifications of sponsor, persons on the premises

Licensure - denial, suspension, or revocation

License fees

Discrimination prohibited

Persons subject to licensing
Persons not subject to licensing

Capacity

Sponsor's resources

Sponsor's absence from home

Effect of local ordinances

Fire safety

Corporal punishment and physical restraints

Resident's records and information

Reporting of illness, death, injury, epidemic, or adult abuse

Reporting changes in circumstances

Transportation

Clothing

Personal hygiene

Training

BOX 4 (continued)

Site

Telephone

Safety and maintenance

Water safety

Firearms

Storage

Bedrooms

Kitchen facilities

Laundry

Toilets, lavatories, and bathing facilities

Lighting

Pest control

Sewage and liquid wastes

Water supply

Temperature

Ventilation

Resident's rights--services to be provided

Health care plan

First aid

Medications controlled by the sponsor

Self-administration of medications

Infection control, communicable disease

Food services

In a quality residential home, all the people (owners, residential care residents, and children) living under one roof act as if they are one family. The purpose is not merely to make money. Rather, residential home operators are in a unique position to provide what is best for the clients.

Residential care home operators have many opportunities to help the elderly retain their independence, to care for themselves, and to make individual and independent decisions. Elderly residents may participate in the care of pets, plants, and gardens; they may get out of doors, and be integrated into activities. Residential homes also permit the elderly to keep their own belongings and to have choices.[10]

Residential care (shelter homes or adult foster care homes) are less restrictive and provide more freedom than nursing homes. The former can revitalize and retain interests of the elderly. (See Box 5.)

According to Gunn (1988), many of the design features and interior components that foster independent living for older individuals provide greater convenience and safety. Some of these include use of ramps, wider doorways, larger bathrooms, walk-in, sit-down showers, electrical outlets at a convenient height and door levers — to name a few. Gunn states, "With imagination and good sense, the dwellings built today could become functional and cherished homes where people can continue to live during their last years."

SOURCES OF FUNDING

Because the aim of this publication is to assist individuals in assessing their interests in and abilities to establish profit-making residential care home businesses for elderly individuals, the sources of funding will concentrate on private funding.

Through *PRIVATE* funding, individuals or families directly pay for the services received in the respective residential care environment.

Another form of individual, private payment is the *TRUST FUND*. In fact, research for this project revealed that many residential home owners found this system to be most efficient. Trust funds are managed through banks or other financial institutions and the actual trust fund payment process is automatic and regulated.

BOX 5

FOOD SERVICES, FACILITIES AND PERSONAL CARE

Food Service is of foremost importance because of the day-to-day sanitation necessary for the prevention

of disease. The food service area, water supply, and preparation area must be totally separate from

bath/laundry water and service areas. Additionally, eating and food service bring a great deal of pleasure

to the elderly. Facilities are critical because of the number of people per room. Safety, storage and access

are all determined here. The best places I observed had two people to a room, all space on one floor, and

easy access to outdoor areas. In each case, the resident elderly were able to maintain and display their

own belongings. Personal care was a concern because most elderly need help with bathing, dressing, etc.

BOX 5 (continued)

Many elderly have denture problems or poor dental health which makes eating a problem. However, this
is even more reason to provide well cooked food, and food choices in a family-style setting.

Social support is vital. Just because people are elderly is no sign they have fewer social needs. If
anything they need more social stimulation. If your elderly residential home members never talk, interact,
or express any independence, then you probably do not have a quality service--in spite of the fact that you
may actually meet your respective state standards.

Consider the fact that social behaviors which appear to determine quality usually go beyond the letter-of-
the-law yet do not add to costs. If anything, they can reduce costs.

One form of federal funds which could be useful is *VETERAN'S BENEFITS*. Again research identified several cases where the basic veteran's support was supplemented by private funds for those veterans living in private residential care homes.

Medicaid is a federal source of funding and an alternative, but the current amount allotted each eligible Medicaid client (approximately $524 per month) which may vary from state to state, fails to provide a level of profit to warrant legitimate income for owners. Interviews with individual residential home owners verified this cost/benefit factor. Note however, residential home operators may accept clients who are receiving Medicare, Social Security insurance and state assistance or a combination of these and also require an additional payment from the family. In some states if the family pays the additional amount directly to the facility, it may not be counted as income for the individual and, therefore, will not affect his or her benefits.[11]

According to Smith, Willis, and Weber (1987), of the three major U.S. personal income categories, transfer payments or third party (SS, Veterans, Medicaid and Medicare) are the fastest growing and in real terms registered a 313 percent increase between 1962 and 1984. One form of transfer payment is that which classified as "retirement and related" — or income payments to persons not currently rendering services. However, transfer payments constitute a larger share of a comparatively smaller pie for the nation's nonmetropolitan areas.

Not only do these funds mean income for residential home operators, but they also constitute a substantial and increasing source of purchasing power for consumer goods and services — with ultimate impact for local growth and development.

For loans, contact your local Small Business Administration (SBA) office. The SBA guarantees $2.8 billion in loans to small businesses. However, if the SBA guarantees your loan, a bank is also likely to lend you money.

COST/BENEFIT FACTORS

While the discussion of economics in the cost/benefit formula is of paramount importance, other subjective cost-benefit variables must also be considered. The nature of the residential home suggests that the main objective of such a business is to make money with which to support the family, the older couple, or perhaps a widowed individual. However, it is often chosen as an income-generating alternative because a homeowner wishes to share an existing home environment or to extend traditional, family-oriented values to others. Specifically, these values include extended family settings, the desire to have the mother remain at home as the primary caretaker of the home and family members, good meals served family style, and the promotion activities which allow young, middle age, and older individuals to interact and have concern for each other (Hall, 1988).[12]

Emotional Factors

Major emotional considerations are both positive and negative. The fact that a family can choose to build a business that can enhance the stability of that respective family is positive. Also, personality factors relative to one's philosophy of life as actualized by caring for other people can be fulfilled. In a residential home business, you must be prepared to give extensive personal attention to your clients, especially at mealtime, during the early morning dressing activities, and at bedtime. You will also need to be prepared to promote socializing activities for those clients who need or want to be involved. Family members of your clients may also expect to make unannounced visits (ACLI, 1989). "Stress" or "burnout" may develop from having to be continuously "on call." The answer to this emotional cost factor is, first, to recognize that it could and does exist and, subsequently, to implement alternatives to combat stress. These options include using respite care assistance and applying stress reduction activities to one's own person or personal environment.[13]

Suggested activities to reduce personal stress are available, often without charge, through numerous sources, one being the local USDA cooperative extension office. Each person has different activities which serve as stress reducers. The important thing is to follow through and perform these on a regular basis.

From an overall viewpoint, attending support groups, asking for help, having back-ups, and using good information sources can all be helpful to you, as a caregiving residential home owner, when combatting stress and fatigue (Jones, 1988).

Financial Factors

The average cost per month for a person to live in a residential home is $1,000. Through interviews with individuals who actually operated residential homes, the author found a minimum of $875 to a maximum of $1,500 per month for each elderly client. Generally speaking, residential care environments are much less costly than nursing home environments. Variables, to name a few, that would greatly influence the cost are the following:

- single, double or triple room occupancy;
- general economic situation of individuals/communities;
- facility's cost/mortgage situation;
- utilities;
- taxes;
- level and quality of social activities;
- number and types of services included;
- availability of registered nurses, emergency care or physical therapist;
- availability of transportation to churches, movies, shopping, etc.

Chapter 3

Business Management

PRELIMINARY ASSESSMENT

The most crucial problem you will face after expressing an interest in starting a new business will be determining if the concept is feasible for you. Too many entrepreneurs strike out on business ventures so convinced of the prospect's merits that they fail to thoroughly evaluate potential benefits and limitations.[14]

Gather, analyze, and evaluate information with the purpose of answering one question: "Should I go into this business?" For a prospective residential home care owner, answering this question involves an assessment of both personal and business considerations. Potential benefits include the feeling of accomplishment, independence in defining your own role in life, and hopefully building greater security for your family. On the other hand, disadvantages will be a loss of personal freedom, confinement and long hours.

Though untrained entrepreneurs have traditionally had high rates of failure, *small businesses can be profitable*. But success in a small home based business is not an accident. It requires both service delivery skills, as well as management and attitudinal competencies.

Personal Characteristics

A variety of business and social scientists have documented research which indicates that successful small business entrepreneurs have some common characteristics. To determine how you measure up, use the checklist below. Write "Y" if you believe the statement describes you, "N" if it doesn't, and "U" if you can't decide:

_____ have a strong desire to be my own boss;

_____ want to be master of my own financial destiny;

_____ have significant specialized business ability based on both education and experience;

_____ have an ability to conceptualize the whole of a business, not just its individual parts, but how they relate to each other;

_____ have developed an inherent sense of what is "right" for a business and have the courage to pursue it;

_____ have one or both parents that were entrepreneurs; calculated risk-taking runs in the family;

_____ live a life characterized by a willingness and capacity to persevere;

_____ possess a high level of energy, sustainable over long hours to make the business successful.

While not every successful home based business owner starts with "Y" answers to all of these questions, three or four "N"s and "U"s should be sufficient reason for you to stop and give second thought to establishing your own business.

Questions in Box 6 ask you to do a little introspection to judge your ability to manage stress. Are your personality characteristics such that you can both adapt to and enjoy residential care small business ownership and management (Ashley and Arnold, 1986)?

Residential Home Self-Review

The following are questions which the potential residential home operator can investigate to clarify further the opportunity for success:

1. What services do you expect to deliver?
2. What fee schedules do you expect to establish?
3. Are there enough clients to fill your expected establishment?
4. How many clients do you need on a continuing basis to remain financially solvent?
5. On what information do you base this expectation?

6. What are the conditions that could change this estimate?
7. How will you promote your business?
8. Why should older people or their families purchase your residential home care services?

Exercises for further assessment:

1. Outline the staff or helpers that will be necessary to maintain your business.
2. Describe your facilities and location of your home (e.g., floor plan, number of bedrooms available, bathrooms, kitchen, laundry, etc.). Compare your original description with an alternative plan developed after completing the additional questions below.
3. Determine whether the building and room arrangements promote independence and privacy.
4. Assess whether you would allow some personal furnishings of the client, such as a favorite chair, to be brought in.
5. Assess whether you are willing to install grab bars and handrails in bathrooms and hallways.
6. Write a statement of philosophy (the values that you stand for) for your new business.

Information in Box 7 can provide further guidance, particularly about the use of your own home for the business.

BUSINESS ORGANIZATION: DEFINING PARAMETERS

This section is suggested for a small proprietorship or family business and will help you conceptualize the actual business. State your response in writing; adjust each area of concern to correspond with your unique needs.

BOX 6

INTROSPECTIVE QUESTIONS

	Yes	No
1. Do you like to make your own decisions?	—	—
2. Do you enjoy setting goals and working toward this goal?	—	—
3. Do you have will power and self-discipline?	—	—
4. Can you take advice from others?	—	—
5. Are you adaptable to changing conditions?	—	—
6. Do you understand that owning your own business may entail working 12 to 16 hours a day, probably seven days a week?	—	—
7. Do you have the physical stamina to handle a business?	—	—
8. Are you prepared to lower your income for several months or years?	—	—
9. Do you know which skills and areas of expertise are critical to the success of your project?	—	—

10. Do you have these skills?

11. Does your idea effectively utilize your own skills and abilities?

12. Can you find personnel that have the expertise you lack?

13. Do you know why you are considering this project?

14. Will your project effectively meet your aspirations?

15. Do you like working with people?

16. Do you like older people?

17. Do you like to cook?

18. Can you give up some privacy in your home environment?

19. Can you facilitate social interaction?

20. Can you tolerate incontinence and/or wandering?

21. Can you tolerate verbal abuse?

22. Can you manage medications?

BOX 7

HOME USE QUESTIONS AND SUGGESTIONS

Questions:

1. Can my current home be used?

2. What changes will be required?

3. What will changes cost?

4. Is the location convenient? (e.g. few steps, parking, etc.)

5. Does it have parking?

6. Is there personal convenience? (e.g.,ground floor)

7. Are utilities adequate?

8. What is the quality and availability of police and fire stations?

9. Are the facilities physically attractive?

<u>Suggestions:</u>

1. Make sure TV, radio and telephones are accessible, as well as books, magazines, reading lamps, call bells, water pitcher, drinking glasses, clocks, and calendars.

2. Avoid stairs and elevated door sills. If these can't be avoided, install a ramp.

3. Make the rooms colorful and homelike.

4. Bathrooms should be as close to the bedrooms as possible.

5. Eliminate shag carpets, slick floors, and scatter rugs to minimize falls.

6. Make sure lighting is bright and adequate in rooms and hallways.

7. If your clients are hard of hearing, install an amplifier on the phone and turn the phone buzzer on "loud."

8. Install adhesive strips to the bathtub and shower to prevent slipping.

9. Place a bench in the bathtub or shower to facilitate easier use for some clients.

10. Wrist straps can be made for walkers and canes to prevent dropping.

11. Change door handles to lever style rather than a knob to facilitate a firmer grip.

12. Use plastic covers to protect a bed if the client is incontinent. Add a mattress pad over the plastic for comfort.

13. Enlarge handles of utensils and tools for those clients who have trouble gripping. Use velcro, foam, rubber, etc. (AARP, 1985).

Part I. — Business Organization

Cover Page:

A. Business Name:

Street Address:

Mailing Address:

Telephone number:

Owner(s) Name(s):

Inside Pages:

B. Business Form:
(proprietorship, partnership, incorporation; most likely, you will be a sole proprietor.)

If your arrangement is other than a sole proprietorship, include copies of necessary key subsidiary documents in an appendix. Remember even partnerships require written agreements of terms and conditions to avoid conflicts and establish legal entities and equities. Corporations require charters, articles of incorporation, and by-laws.

Part II. — Business Purpose and Function

In this section write an accurate but concise description of the business. Describe, in narrative form, the business you plan to start.

The principal service. Be specific.

How will it be started?

- a new startup?
- when?

Why will it succeed? Be positive and promote your idea!

- what is unique about your business?
- what are the special features?

What is your experience in this business? If you have a current resume, include it in an appendix. If you lack specific experience, detail how you plan to obtain it, such as training, an apprenticeship, or working with an experienced partner (Eliason, 1983).[15]

Part III. — Organizational Information

1. Design a simple organizational chart. If you will operate a family-run business, this will identify who will be responsible for which tasks (see Figure 1).
2. Describe or outline the duties and responsibilities of each.
3. List other resource individuals such as attorneys, accountants, Area Office of Aging ombudsman, state offices in charge of standards, etc.

4. List other outside resources that are available free of charge; for instance, both SCORE and ACE help small business owners solve their operating problems. Check contract information through the yellow pages for those community bound organizations. Also, the U. S. Small Business Administration Office of Business Development will provide resource materials.

Personnel

While most small family-run residential homes or adult foster care businesses fulfill their own staffing needs, there may be a point at which other personnel will need to be hired. One or two people, which are usually a husband/wife team, can care for four to six patients. Beyond this, the pair will probably need assistance.[16]

Options for getting respite include: (1) hiring an assistant, (2) periodically employing an outside "respite care" worker, or (3) calling upon other family members to serve in assistant roles.

Respite Care

Respite care is the temporary relief for caregivers from the demand of in-home patient care. Fundamentally, a respite worker is a substitute caretaker trained to assume responsibility in the absence of the residential care operator. This substitute is called a "Respite Worker."[17]

Individuals hired to provide respite assistance may be available through hospitals or home health agencies. Or operators may hire other independent workers as respite assistants. One of the community service systems growing out of the increased growth of residential homes or adult foster homes is the *respite care referral system*. Though it does not exist in many communities or states, the purpose of the system is to maintain an area registry of respite care workers or those who can serve as short-time care assistants. The clearinghouse not only provides a directory of persons but also functions as a self-enforced evaluator of respite workers. Should a person not perform well, the networking system would automatically become aware of the situation; likewise, should an individual perform extremely well, this information would work through the system.

Respite care clearinghouses that I observed were managed by

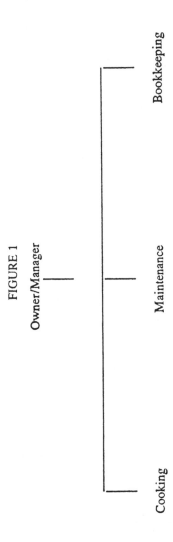

FIGURE 1

Owner/Manager

Cooking

Maintenance

Bookkeeping

volunteers, but for effectiveness in the future, they could and should become institutionalized within the Health and Human Service Systems.

The respite period may be for a few days to a few weeks. Each business or agency may have a different set of rules regarding respite service. Well in advance of requiring this sort of assistance, an owner should call the agency or worker for specific information.

(NOTE: The Medicare Catastrophic Act, effective January 1, 1990, will provide up to 80 hours per year of in-home respite care paid relief for care-givers who reach the Part B catastrophic cap or the prescription drug deductible and care of the deductible for chronically dependent individuals. This will continue to change.)

It will always be important to orient and provide clear instructions for your assistant, especially if you are away from the premises.

Emergency information should be posted in an obvious place and should be clearly available for respite workers, as well as for providers. (See Box 8.)[18]

Hired Regular Help

Specific characteristics an employer can look for in a potential employee are enthusiasm, expressed interest in the elderly, reliability and honesty. Personnel must care for family valuables, must be energetic, be able to think quickly, and be willing to take initiative. Interviews with residential home operators indicated that most paid employees wages from $4.00 to $5.50 per hour, depending on performance and how long they had worked for the employers. All home business operators interviewed for this project also suggested that personnel be expected to show affection for and interest in the elderly. These particular behaviors can be observed. The following steps may be taken:

1. Have potential employee complete a regular personnel application form.
2. Conduct an interview with the potential employee. Ask questions about his or her interest in the elderly and experiences in working or living on a daily basis with the elderly.
3. Plan a one-day work observation/experience where you have

the prospective employee participate in all aspects of day-to-day care for the elderly. This should include all tasks required of an employee such as food service and bathing. They should keep notes, write down comments, questions, etc.
4. Conduct a follow-up interview after the work experience.
5. Plan the first week on a probationary basis. During this time, observe the worker as you integrate him or her into all daily tasks. Allow time for the worker to discuss experiences and for you to give feedback.
6. Determine the employee's willingness to learn about elderly people, to learn medical terminology, prescription terms and other language pertinent to the elderly.

After an employee is hired to be an assistant, an opportunity should be provided for the employee to relate to a doctor before being left alone or given extensive responsibility with the elderly clients. As the employer, you should obtain feedback from the doctor about this employee.

After all training and hiring is complete, the business will have invested approximately $1,000. Therefore, it is important to give great care to the hiring process and, once the employee is hired, to treat him or her positively so as to prevent turnover. Positive steps can include verbal compliments, mention in newsletters or in written communication to families of the elderly clients, merit pay raises or bonuses, and integration in more decision making — to name a few.

The advantages of having a regular employee are several: such employment instigates contributions to long-term Social Security benefits system; regular work gives the employee a sense of belonging to an ongoing, stable working situation, as well as increased opportunity to contribute to the "caretaker" profession; regular work also motivates the employee with the possibility of earning regular pay raises with continued service. (See Box 9.)

Disadvantages for the employee include the extra responsibility of being reliable and dependable — keeping regular hours, etc., a few less dollars in actual take home pay (due to social security deductions), and quite possibly, the requisite of additional training.

For employees, advantages of working on a consultant basis are

BOX 8

SAMPLE OF INSTRUCTIONS FOR RESPITE WORKERS

MILLIE: Does not drink milk, does not care for pork. Wears night-time plastic pant and liner. These are located on shelf in her closet. She dresses self. Sometimes confused and needs help. HALLUCINATES. Encourage her to drink liquids. She needs to be reminded to urinate before bedtime. She is shy about using the toilet. Help her to find the door and tell her to "try" particularly if she has not been to the bathroom in 3 or 4 hours. TAXES 2 AVENTYL after dinner. If you give them at bedtime she has hard time waking up in A.M.

CARRIE: Dresses self and does own hygiene care. Takes Dyazide and Synthroid at lunch and Dyazide at dinner. She will self-medicate.

ROBERTA: Can not eat pork or gravy. Dresses self and does own hygiene. She may want to bathe. Give her clean towel and washcloth. Help her find clean underwear. She will select her own clothes. She is afraid someone will take her clothes, so let her put her dirties in her closet. I'll wash them later. Watch her take her pills: one Mellaril at noon and one Mellaril with one amitriptyline at 7:00 P.M. If she experiences chest pain, give her a Reglan as needed (too many will cause diarrhea); for headaches give her two aspirin; for eye pain a drop of Visine; for bad hip give her aspirin.

DOGS AND CATS: Food in storeroom next to Milene's room. We feed them in the morning. Housecat fed in the laundry room. Outside cat fed in garage. Freckles fed by back door. Amount of food to be given each animal is posted inside the storeroom door. Dippers for other animals in the food bins. On these hot days I give dogs cool water after lunch. FRECKLES SLEEPS IN HOUSE.

BOX 8 (continued)

KITCHEN: Please do not put knives with wood handles in the dishwasher. I wash and dry and replace on chopping block. I only run dishwasher when it is full. Set on quick wash and fill 1 soap cup. (Usually I have pre-rinsed all the dishes so it is a matter of sterilizing them.) Watch out that Tupperware lids do not get down in bottom. The heating element will melt them.

FOOD: The ladies eat nearly anything. The storeroom is downstairs. You will find nearly anything you might need in the way of soups, vegetables, snacks, or whatever. There is hamburger in the freezer. There is bread in the upstairs freezer. Usually there is ice cream. Potatoes and onions are located in the storeroom by the door and in the bins under the chopping block. Carrots, lettuce, celery, tomatoes are in the refrigerator. (Carrie does not care for lettuce or Miracle Whip on her sandwiches, just a small amount of mustard. The other ladies eat lettuce and Miracle Whip.) All the ladies like peanut butter, pancakes, jelly, eggs, oatmeal, cold cereal, toast, fruit, jello, pudding, etc.

that he or she does not have to be committed to the work environment on a regular basis. Rather he or she can have the opportunity to move to various businesses where entry level skills and knowledge can be enhanced, and the worker can "try-out" an area of interest before committing to longer term employment. For the employer, such arrangements permit testing the worker's basic skills and interests. Disadvantages concentrate on the fact that salary for the worker may not be as great as desired or that it may be earned only on a sporadic basis.

Registered Nurses

On occasion, it may be necessary to hire a registered nurse. For example, in some states, minimum standards will require at least a monthly facilities and program check by a registered nurse. If one of the business owners is not a registered nurse, you may need to formally contract with a nurse of your choice.

Food Service

Of all the services that nurture basic, social needs of the elderly who live with you, of extreme importance is the day-to-day food service. *Eating is still one of the activities that brings a great deal of pleasure to the elderly.* At the same time, they may have several problems such as chewing or special diet needs that will require special attention.

From interviews with business owners, it appears that quality traditional family food service is most popular. Owners shopped weekly and maintained regular shopping lists. At times, some of the elderly individuals had special requests for food items or favorite snacks. Prior to the shopping day, their requests were added to the list.

Food costs will be one of the highest expenses, but quality of nutrition and food preparation *must be maintained.* (See Box 10.)

State standards will likely require that you maintain menus and that you have these evaluated regularly by a nutritionist. You might request the services of the county extension Home Economist, or you can hire a private nutritionist. Training programs conducted by the State Department of Health should be helpful in gaining addi-

BOX 9

SAMPLE FORM:
INDIVIDUAL CONTRACTOR/RESPITE WORKER

This is to certify that I, _____, am accepting employment at _____ per hour on a contract basis.

Therefore, I am responsible, accordingly, for paying any benefits or taxes.

If I earn more than $600 per year, the person/agency from whom I received these funds will provide me with a federal W-2 account.

_____ date

Contractor

_____ date

Business mgr/owner

tional knowledge and skills in relation to food sanitation, food safety, nutrition, etc.

Basic guidelines for food preparation should definitely include an emphasis on nutrition. While the statement "You are what you eat," may be true, older people may need to change "What they eat." Although most older people need the same nutrition as younger people, some, if they are less active, may need fewer calories. Or they may have special diet needs. For example, if a client has high blood pressure, his or her doctor may recommend the individual cut down on salt and sodium. Or sugar might be reduced for some to lose weight. However, do not make serious changes in any patient's diet without first consulting the client's doctor.

Planning meals consists of combining the essential food groups in the right proportions and in wholesome, attractive ways. Attractive meal service is not dependent upon elaborate and expensive table appointments; rather, it is the social aspect of the meal which is vital. Mealtimes are the time of day when people who live together spend regular time interacting with each other.

Market lists are best written from planned menus, but the menus should be flexible to take advantage of particular bargain foods within each group when shopping. These food groups are fruits and vegetables; whole-grain and enriched breads, cereals and other products made from grains; milk, cheese, yogurt, and other products made from milk; and meats, poultry, fish, eggs, dry beans and peas.

To enhance meals, other factors that need consideration are flavor, color, shape of foods and method of preparation. Too many sweet foods or too many sour foods in the same meal affect the palatability of the foods. The repetition of flavors or the same food in the meal should be avoided. As well, distinctive flavors must be used with discretion.

Textures (soft, hard, chewy, crisp) and shapes (round, long, flat, diced) of foods also need to be varied. If a meal is composed entirely of white or neutral-colored foods, it is probably uninteresting. If color can be introduced without marring the flavor or texture, and it usually can be, a much more appetizing meal will be the result.

It is never desirable to use an excess of foods that are rich in fat and sugar, but more of these foods are used in winter. Even in warm

BOX 10

GOALS FOR MEAL PLANNING

1. The provision of nutritionally adequate diets for family members of all ages.

2. The matching of meals with the family food budget.

3. The consideration of individual preferences, traditions, and cultures.

4. The efficient management of the time, energy and materials available.

weather, some warm foods are desirable, and in cold months, some cool foods should be included in the menus. During warm weather, one must guard to see that protein needs are met. People tend to serve lighter, non-protein vegetable-salad type meals in warm months (Bennion, 1980; Merrock, 1985).

For older individuals, more emphasis needs to be put on softer, more easily chewed casseroles, fewer highly spiced foods and more bulk or heavy fiber foods.

As the employer in charge of all food purchasing, you will want to consider the following:

1. Food labels, which provide a great deal of information concerning what you're getting, e.g., nutritional content, ingredients, grade, code or shelf life.
2. Nutrition per serving basis, including USRDA (U.S. Recommended Daily Allowances) of calories, protein, vitamins and minerals.
3. Unit Pricing, which is a quick and easy way to make unit price comparisons at a glance. The unit price label provides you with a brand name, a description of the product, the size of the package, the retail price (the price you pay) and the unit price, which is the price per measure or unit (AARP, 1985). Your County Extension Home Economists can also supply you with a copy of the U.S. Department of Agriculture, Health and Human Services Dietary Guidelines for Americans (1985). As well, they can recommend training, networking, and other important nutrition and food service contact information.

For more information concerning nutritional health, contact the following:

1. Consumer Affairs Office
   The Food and Drug Administration
   HFE-88
   5600 Fishers Lane
   Rockville, MD 20857
2. Human Nutrition Information Service
   U.S. Department of Agriculture

6505 Belcrest Road
Hyattsville, MD 20782
3. Local Cooperative Extension Home Economists
   USDA Cooperative Extension

REGULATIONS

Health Inspections

Most states will require some level of periodic inspections by licensing, health and/or medical personnel. For example, a registered nurse may visit on a monthly basis to check medications, care plans, etc. The Nurse Consulting Agreement Form can be used with this procedure.

Legal and Community Considerations

You will want to investigate potential legal and community problems associated with operating the business from home. You should gather, read, and understand respective state residential home facility laws and standards.

Check first! Get facts in writing. Keep a topical file for future reference. Some facts and forms will be needed for your business plan, for example, census data, zoning laws or regulations, remodeling plans or drawings, and cost estimates. Clip and store these in your business topical file. Then be sure to compare your plans with state standards because there may be limitations enforced that can make your planned business impossible or require expensive modifications to your property. Call or visit the county or city zoning office to check on restrictions, if any (Schnarl et al., 1989).

The federal government has also enacted two bills that spell out the rights of long-term care clients, one of these being specifically for intermediate care facilities such as residential care homes. These can also provide you with insight into legal management situations and you may want to consider providing the choice of having your clients develop and maintain a living will (AARP, 1988).

RESIDENTS:
CONSIDERING CLIENTS AND THEIR NEEDS

Residential Population

Since you will probably service a very limited number of people (2-8), it may not be difficult to recruit your population, but you still need to consider the factors listed below:

1. What is the geographic area you can expect to cover?
2. What is the population of elderly in these areas?
3. Are there other individuals who potentially can use your services (e.g., developmentally disabled)?
4. What do you know about the population growth of those individuals classified as elderly?
5. What is the per-capita income of the elderly?
6. Does the price you expect to charge in keeping with the area per-capital income?
7. Is your potential large enough to fit your profit needs?
8. Do you have competition? If so, what are the major strengths and major weaknesses of these competitors? What are yours?
9. Can you compete with other similar area businesses?
10. Do you know your competitor's profit schedule?
11. Do you know if your competitors plan to expand?
12. Can you describe the type of client your business can and cannot service? What criteria will you use for selecting your clients?

Recruitment

There are some primary ways for residential home operators to recruit or enroll elderly clients. Some states (e.g., Nevada) but not all, have data clearinghouse offices that provide referrals. Some states have informal clearinghouse systems managed by Residential Home Owner Associations (e.g., Washington). The most likely place to get this type of information is through the State or Area Offices on Aging or the Association of Residential Care Owners. (See Box 11.)

BOX 11

RECRUITMENT STRATEGIES

— Use "word of mouth" contacts in social or religious circles. Families or groups you relate to through club or church activities often will know of individuals who could benefit from your residential home. Most of the private residential home operators interviewed recruited their members through this system.

— Use contacts with or references from medical doctors.

— Network with the state association of "residential home" operators. Note: If your state does not have such an association, you might consider starting one.

— Network with an Office on Aging ombudsman who will understand the local population and may be aware of individual needs. However, this person may only know of those on his or her respective list.

— Advertise in the newspaper.

— Advertise in the yellow pages.

— Develop flyers and hand-out materials.

Specific Responsibilities

The following lists indicate items, outside of space, furnishings, meals, and utilities, for which the residential care owner and families, respectively, were responsible:

Residential Home Owner	Resident or his/her family
Kleenex	trips to physician*
creams and lotions	get prescriptions and deliver to residential home
soap	clothes
laundry services	personal items
toothpaste	transportation
shampoo	

All owners interviewed maintained "No Smoking" policies. Given that common problems of the elderly are often respiratory related, a no smoking policy is understandable.

Criteria for Recruiting and Selecting Clients

Sample criteria for recruiting and selecting clients may be found in Box 12.

Policies

Most owners interviewed had a two week trial clause in their contracts which gives the owner/operator an opportunity to determine if there is a match between what the client needs and what the owner/operator has to offer or whether the client's requisites can be fulfilled in a home environment. One month's advance deposit should be required with a clear statement in the contract about refund conditions.

An individual plan of care designed to meet the needs of each person is maintained as a normal part of record keeping in residen-

---

* One owner did take individuals to physicians — indicating she believed her regular auto liability coverage protected her.

BOX 12

SAMPLE CRITERIA FOR RECRUITING

AND SELECTING CLIENTS

1. Ambulatory

2. Does not smoke

3. Hearing is reasonably good

4. Comprehends and understands directions

5. Is oriented to reality

6. Is continent

7. Can bathe and dress self

8. Can communicate verbally

tial homes. The plan takes into consideration the older person's physical, social and psychological needs and is designed to maintain the person at, or restore him or her to, optimal capability for self-care.

The policies you establish on behalf of your business will be instrumental for the initial public-relations image. Secondly, they will facilitate recruitment and permit the management to function more smoothly — perhaps preventing serious legal problems later. Always of great importance is the practice of being "up-front" with potential clients and their families about your residential home business policies. These should be established in a written format so they can be shared.

Factors to consider in setting policies could include safety, your own interests and limitations, legal concerns, consideration of what items you want to be responsible for, what you want the client and/or the client's family to be responsible for and the Federal Intermediate Care Bill of Rights. The Bill of Rights generally covers areas of:

- All rules governing resident conduct;
- Receipt of rules;
- Information in writing about costs and charges;
- Opportunity to participate in planning;
- Opportunity to refuse treatment;
- Written consent for participation in experimental research;
- Transfer and discharge;
- Opportunity to exercise rights as a citizen;
- Opportunity to manage own financial offices;
- Owner compliance with record keeping;
- Resident must be free from mental and physical abuse;
- Resident must be free from physical restraints unless caretaker has authorization;
- Resident must be treated with consideration, respect, and dignity;
- Resident data must be treated with confidentiality;
- A married resident must be given privacy when visited by a spouse;
- Husband and wife, if both are residents, must be allowed to share a room;

- Each resident must be allowed to send and receive mail, and to participate in social, religious and community group activities;
- Maintenance of personal belongings as space permits.

Some management areas that could be included in policy statements are the following:

- House rules or those situations pertaining to storage and possession of valuables.
- Visits of outside members and friends.
- Conditions under which clients will need to discontinue living in your Residential Care home. This might include physician's recommendation that the client needs a level of service above what you can provide. Or the individual may need to move if he or she is capable of living independently.
- No smoking conditions, based on health and safety factors.
- Probationary periods.
- Possession of large amounts of money.
- Possession of expensive jewelry.

Contracts

Alternate short contract format may be found in Box 13.

Care Plans

Individual Care Plans will be required. While a statement of the situations under which individuals come to live in your home is rudimentary, it should be updated with running comments, such as visits to the doctors, changes in conditions, etc. Other more formal systems may be required by some states, but each individual's file should, as a minimum, include basic information:

- Doctor's name and phone numbers,
- Relative's name and phone numbers,
- Hospital,
- Interests and hobbies,
- Favorite foods,
- Special needs (e.g., interest in belonging),
- Brief past individual and/or family history,

- Medication information,
- Funeral home information, if available.

All medications can be kept in a specially designed "prescription box," approximately 18″ × 18″ and 3-4″ deep and separated into small boxed spaces approximately 2″ × 4″, or big enough to hold one prescription container. On the left of the rows, each client's name can be entered and across the top, times or periods of the day can be labeled (i.e., B, L, D, BT). This is designed so it can (1) be locked and (2) serve each client's special prescription medication needs. Only those medications as prescribed by the respective physicians are kept here.

BOX 13

ALTERNATE SHORT CONTRACT FORMAT*

CONTRACT TO PROVIDE ADULT FAMILY HOME SERVICES

COMMENCING _____ day of _____, 19 ____, the Adult Family Home _____ agrees to provide all the services including room and board on a month to month basis to _____. In return for her/his care and supervision the sum of $ _____ will be paid in advance by the resident or the resident's legal guardian to the Adult Family Home on the _____ day of every month for the following month.

The Adult Family Home reserves the right to increase the amount of compensation in cases where the care of the resident continues to increase with the passage of time. The resident or legal guardian shall remain responsible for damages caused by _____ beyond normal wear. This includes abusive behavior to premises and furnishings and damages from loss of bladder or bowel control. Either party may terminate this agreement with a 14-day written notice.

The undersigned agrees to the preceding conditions:

_____
Adult Family Home   date

_____
Resident   date

_____
Legal Guardian   date

*You may wish to design and use a longer more detailed format.

Chapter 4

Financial Aspects

PROJECTIONS

Success/Failure Variables

To determine whether your idea meets the basic requirements for a successful new project, you must be able to answer at least one of the following questions with a "yes":

1. Does your service provide an unserved need?
2. Does the business serve an existing market in which demand exceeds supply?
3. Can you successfully compete with existing competition because of an "advantageous situation," such as better price, location, etc.?

A "Yes" response to questions such as the following would indicate that the idea has less chance for success:

1. Are there any pieces of important information unavailable (e.g., zoning)?
2. Are money (capital) requirements excessive for establishing your business?
3. Is adequate financing difficult to obtain?
4. Would potential problems prevent obtaining certification or a license?
5. Are there factors that prevent effective recruitment?

ESTIMATING INCOME AND EXPENSES

Desired Income

The following questions should remind you that you must have both a return on your business investment as well as a reasonable salary for the time you spend in operating that business:

1. How much income do you desire?
2. Are you prepared to earn less income in the first 1-3 years?
3. What minimum income do you require?
4. What financial investment will be required for your business?
5. How much could you earn by investing this money?
6. How much could you earn by working for someone else?
7. Add the amounts in 5 and 6. If this income is greater than what you can realistically expect from your business, are you prepared to forego this additional income in order to be your own boss with only the prospects of more substantial profit/income in future years?
8. What is the average return on investment for a business of your type?

Expenses

1. What will rent or mortgage expenses be?
2. What will general food costs be?
3. What will utility costs be?
4. What will insurance costs be?

CONFRONTING RISKS

1. What are the major risks associated with your business?
2. How can you minimize these major risks?
3. Which of these risks can you control? How?
4. Could these risks bankrupt you?

THE FINANCIAL PLAN

Clearly the most critical section of your business plan document is the financial plan. In formulating this, you will establish vital information that will guide the financial health of your business through the first year and beyond.

While your residential home service may improve the condition of mankind for generations to come, you will fail if you don't make a profit. If you don't know what's going on in your business, you are not in a very good position to assure its profitability. There are, therefore, some very basic processes for which you need to be prepared.

Before initially operating your business, you need to decide who will keep the records, yourself or someone else. Frequently the individual business owner will keep the books. This arrangement gives you a better understanding of what is happening in the business by keeping you current. Also, you become very familiar with the system. Sometimes an employee, a spouse or other family member, or an outside bookkeeping or accounting service will do the record keeping. This is usually satisfactory if the individual is qualified, keeps the books current, and keeps you informed. Regardless of who keeps the records, you must review them periodically to know what is going on and how the business is doing.[19]

All too often, the only motivation for keeping records is for tax purposes. This is important, of course, but overall your records should be able to do the following:

- Show you how much profit you are making;
- Illustrate the financial condition of your business;
- Provide a basis for decision making;
- Give you information necessary to complete the required income tax forms.

The key to an effective, efficient bookkeeping system is to set it up correctly in the first place. It must have the following characteristics:

1. simple to use,
2. easy to understand,
3. reliable,
4. accurate,
5. consistent,
6. designed to provide information on a timely basis.

You do not need an elaborate system for a small business. Most home businesses operating on a cash basis use a common single-entry system for income and outgo.[20]

There are a number of one-write, duplicate check, and pegboard systems available commercially. Some are prepared with instructions and forms designed for specific kinds of businesses; others are for small-business use in general. You can examine some of these systems at office supply stores. In addition, some trade associations, manufacturers, and wholesalers offer specially designed recordkeeping systems to their members or customers. The SBA publication, "Recordkeeping Systems," (SBA, 115A) lists many such systems. You can get a free copy of it from *U.S. Small Business Administration, P.O. Box 15434, Fort Worth, TX 76119.*

The simplest system for all financial transactions is to record them in your business checkbook. *All expenditures* should be paid for by checks drawn on an account kept strictly for the business. Set up a petty cash fund for small business expenses with a check drawn on the business account.

Use a check register that allows enough space to enter information to determine later what money represents income and what money represents personal funds or loans deposited. Pioneer Business Forms prints several check and deposit register forms under the brand name Ekonomik. The form is set up with expense columns to the left and check, deposit, and balance columns to the right. For a complete checkbook, register forms can be combined with binders and checks. Binders come equipped with a special metal strap for holding previously used register pages. (Ekonomik style checks can be ordered through your bank or from Ekonomik Systems, Box 11413, Tacoma, WA 98411, and inserted into the binders. The self-carbonizing kind are most useful.)

Payments for inventory, supplies, employees' salaries, if any, business travel, rent utilities, and other expenses should be recorded in the check register by date, amount, payee, and purpose. A bank charge is entered in the same manner as a check except that there is no check number. If you must write a check payable to cash or to yourself to pay for a business expense with cash, you should file the receipt for the cash payment in your records. If you cannot get a receipt for a cash payment, put a note explaining the expense in your records at the time of payment.

Every check should have a written document to support it, such as an invoice, a payroll summary, or bill statement. All bills should be checked prior to payment. Invoices should be matched with the goods received (receipt log), and checked for terms, cash discounts and prices. Invoices and bill statements should be marked "Paid," with the date and check number noted to prevent duplicate payouts. These documents should be put into a "paid-bills" file. At the end of the year, you can summarize your profit picture by comparing deposits and expenditures. This system can be combined with other records to give a more complete picture of the business.[21]

You need to reconcile your business checkbook monthly as soon as the bank statement arrives. Before you start to reconcile your monthly bank statement, quickly check your own figures. Begin with the balance shown in your checkbook at the end of the prior month. To this balance add the total cash deposited during the present month and subtract total cash disbursements for the present month. Now go back and be sure that each page of the check register is balanced. Directives for balancing an account are usually also explained on the back of your bank statement.

If, after adding this month's cash deposits and subtracting this month's cash disbursements from last month's checkbook balance, the result does not agree with your statement's balance at the end of the month, check to see if an error was made when entering the number in the "amount of check" column. Check deposit slip copies to be sure that each individual entry tallies with the entry in the checkbook register. If the balance is still off, check to make sure your additions and subtractions are correct. When your checkbook balance agrees with the bank statement, bring forward the previous month's balance to get the totals for the year to date.

SUPPORT RECORDS FOR FINANCIAL SYSTEM

To have an accurate idea of what the business must make or is making, assess your own personal financial statements, tax returns for the past three years, and a personal family budget. This is useful information for calculating financial expectations and is mandatory if you are attempting to secure financing from an outside source. If you are seeking outside financing, you will need to describe the project to be financed, state financial sources for the project, and list the uses for this money. Depreciation allowances for fixed assets such as equipment, furniture, vehicles, etc. will be calculated from the *Source of Funds Schedule.*

To create this schedule, you will need to create a list of all the assets that you intend to use in your business, how much investment each will require and the source of funds to capitalize them. A sample list of items that will likely be considered are shown in Table 3.

After an initial start-up of three to six months, Accounts Receivable Profits can be counted (e.g., 4 clients × $500 profit × 3 mo. = $6,000). Once your assets and costs are itemized, they can be used to develop a financial profile. See format as shown in Box 14.

A number of financial ratios provide information about the financial position of a small business beyond that provided by the absolute dollar values in the balance sheet and income statement. These ratios can be separated into three kinds of information.

TABLE 3

ASSET	COST	SOURCE OF FUNDS
Cash	$2,500	Personal savings
Inventory	2,000	Vendor Credit
Current Home	50,000	Currently owned
Furniture	2,000	Currently owned
Appliances	2,000	Currently owned

BOX 14

FINANCIAL PROFILE FORMAT

A. **SOURCES OF FUNDS** (Add descriptions as needed.)

CASH IN BANKS $ _____

LOANS (balance between value pay-off) $ _____

MORTGAGES $ _____

EQUITY (ownership in properties) $ _____

INVESTMENTS $ _____

TOTAL AVAILABLE CASH $ _____

BOX 14 (continued)

B. **USES OF FUNDS**

PURCHASE OF PROPERTY $ _____

CONSTRUCTION $ _____

CAPITAL GOODS $ _____

INVENTORY $ _____

OPERATING CAPITAL $ _____

OTHER (Loan payments) $ _____

TOTAL $ _____

1. *Balance sheets*, which refer to relationships between various balance sheet items.
2. *Operating ratios*, which show the relationships of expense items to net sales.
3. Information which shows the relationship between an item in the *profit-and-loss statement* and one on the *balance sheet.*[22]

All of this information should be compared over time. A change in a ratio might indicate that there is a problem, but additional analysis is usually needed to determine what action should be taken. Ratios do not provide solutions, but they do alert business people to potential problems.

Besides the checkbook systems other necessary small residential home business records need not be complicated or excessive. In fact, forms that make up minimum recommendations are the following:

• Income Statements
• Balance Sheet
• Cash Flow Projects
• Projected Profit and Loss Statement

Besides a return on investment, you need to know the *income and expenses* for your business. You show *profit or loss* and *derive operating ratios* from this information. Dollars are the amounts for income and expense categories as actual, estimated or those that are residential home averages. Copies of these forms can be obtained from your local bank. Information in Box 14 may serve as a guide for developing a financial profile.

First estimate or forecast income (revenue) and expense dollars and ratios for your business. Then compare your estimated or actual performance with your state or area average. Analyze differences to see why your venture does or doesn't look like it will succeed. Using the model Residential Home Income Statement, forecast your own income statement. Estimates must be *as accurate as possible* or else you will have a false impression.

To continue your exercise in planning, make a copy of the *balance sheet*. Again, you can obtain from your local bank a copy to use as your working draft to get started and transfer the data to another form later.

Even though you may plan to state the purchase of some assets through the year, for the purposes of this sample balance sheet, assume that all assets will be provided at the startup.

In the wide, unnumbered column on the left of your 13-column sheet, list components of your income, cost, and expense structure. You may add or delete specific lines of expense to suit your business plan. Guard against consolidating too many types of expense under one account lest you lose control of the components. At the same time, don't try to break down expenses so discretely that accounting becomes a nuisance instead of a management tool. Headings may be taken from the areas outlined on the Project Cash Flow Form or the Sources of Funds Schedule. This provides ample detail for most home based businesses. Prudent business management practice is to keep no more cash in the business than is needed to operate it and to protect it from catastrophe. In most small businesses, the problem is rarely one of having too much cash. A Cash Flow Projection is made to advise management of the amount of cash that is going to be absorbed by the operation of the business and to compare it against the amount that will be available.

Make copies of these and apply them to your business, first as examples and later as actually applied data. For example, complete the *profit and loss statement* as follows: Write at the top of the first page the planned name of your business. On the second line of the heading, write "Profit and Loss Projection." On the third line, write "First Year." If startup is indefinite, just write "Month #1, Month #2," etc. Column 13 should be headed "Total Year." (See Box 15.)

Questions that can help you work through the process of estimating your finances are the following:

1. What are the normal or average charges for residential home care?
2. What are your fixed costs (e.g., mortgages, etc.)?
3. What is the average cost of expenses (utilities, food, mortgages) as percentage of gross income?

4. What is the average gross profit?
5. What is the average net profit?

Take the preceding figures and work backwards using a standard income statement format to determine the number of clients necessary to support your desired level of income. After your calculations, ask yourself, from a practical standpoint, whether this number of clients, these expenses, and this profit are attainable?

INSURANCE

In a residential care home, business insurance will be one of the most expensive costs, so you will need to make decisions about coverage. Check with your insurance agent for help in insuring against hazards specific to your operation:

- fire, theft and casualty damage,
- liability for customers,
- worker's compensation,
- business use of vehicle coverage.

Note: In interviews with a number of small residential home owners, it was found that operators with four to eight clients carried limited liability insurance. This was based on the rationale that, one, they could not make a profit if they carried complete or comprehensive coverage and, two, if any incident was so serious as to perpetuate a law-suit, owners would probably have to close the business anyway. Given the situation, owners took greater care to protect the elderly individuals. One of the owners, who managed a 22-bed facility, did carry complete liability coverage. This was one of his biggest expenses.

Typically, a basic small-business insurance policy offers more extensive coverage than a homeowner's policy. Aetna, Prudential, the Fireman's Fund and Nationwide are among the insurance companies that offer small-business policies.

BOX 15

RESIDENTIAL HOME MODEL INCOME STATEMENT

(Based on six residential home individuals)

	Amount
Gross income	72,000

Expenses

Food	12,000	
Insurance/attorneys	6,000	
Utilities/maintenance	3,000	
Mortgage	10,000	
Total expenses		31,000
Operating profit		41,000
Other costs	1,200	
Net Profit before taxes		39,800
Taxes (state & fed.)		9,000
Net Profit after taxes		30,800

TAXES

To learn about the income tax regarding a home business, secure the IRS publication *#587, Business Use Of Your Home* through IRS Hotline 1-800-829-3676.

Research for this project revealed that some home care providers deducted employee's share of Social Security and worker's compensation contributions and also paid their employer shares. Primarily these businesses were larger, serving eight to twenty-two clients and requiring additional help on a regular basis. Other small businesses that were predominantly run by family members only hired additional outside workers on an irregular basis.

Some owners hired assistants or "respite care helpers" on what is classified as an individual consultant basis.

Hiring contracts issued by employers should reflect tax status. When employees are hired on a temporary or consultant basis, employers do not pay or withhold Social Security funds, nor do they contribute to unemployment or worker's compensation. For a sole proprietorship the minimum information on an employee record is that required to complete the Federal Internal Revenue Service Form 1040, Schedule C. Other business types (partnerships, joint ventures, corporations) have similar requirements but use different tax forms. However, only if the employee earns more than $600 annually does the employer submit annual W2 forms to each employee and Form 1099 to the federal government. A toll free number for federal tax information and for ordering tax forms is 1-800-424-1040. This number may change depending upon the state. You may need to call 1-800-555-1212 toll free information for your respective state number.

Chapter 5

Support Information

SPECIAL CONCERNS

Rural

Rural America is at a critical juncture. Declines in farmland values, instability of net-farm income, and increased international competition for natural resource-based industries — timber, agriculture, mining, fishing, and petroleum, when combined with the loss of rural manufacturing jobs — threaten the vitality of rural institutions. This makes the crisis a reality for urban and rural Americans, all of whom have a stake in a strong, viable rural America.[23]

The well-being of rural families, both those who are involved in agriculture and those who are not, affects the quality of life in the communities in which they live. Their economic well-being depends upon their purchasing power, income stability, and resource management skills. Physical well-being is related to the availability of basic needs, such as health care and housing, including housing that meets the special needs of the elderly. For social well-being, families must have access to community organizations and resources which provide support.

Revitalizing rural America is a challenge that requires an integrated effort both within the Cooperative Extension System and among many other organizations. Meeting the challenge necessitates that new and different knowledge and research be applied to changing realities for rural people, businesses, and communities. (See Box 16.)[24]

There are many questions about the future of rural America, including its communities and people. Finding answers to these ques-

BOX 16

LONG-TERM SOCIAL AND ECONOMIC CHANGES IN RURAL AMERICA

— change in population which has led to loss of political influence;

— decrease in federal support for rural counties and communities;

— loss of tax bases that cause financial stress in many rural areas;

— rising levels of family stress with consequent social, psychological, and marital disruptions;

— loss of jobs

tions calls for a major research initiative focusing on the complex relations among agriculture, the rural economy, rural families, and rural communities (Lambell et al. 1988).[25]

Urban-Suburban

Today's older persons tend to remain where they have spent most of their adult lives. For both adults and children, rates of moving decline with increasing age. The highest rate of moving is among adults in their early 20s. Between 1983 and 1984, only 4.6 percent of older persons moved, compared to 34.1 percent of 20- to 24-year-olds and 16.8 percent of persons of all ages.

Areas with an exceptionally high proportion of older persons include those to which the older population has relocated in retirement. For example, in 1985, almost half of the country's older population lived in eight states: California, New York, Florida, Pennsylvania, Texas, Illinois, Ohio, and Michigan. Each of these states had over a million persons age 65-plus.

Generally, the urban-suburban environments which support growth in residential care homes for the frail elderly will be influenced by several factors. One, the employment sector is moving toward more service systems and there will be more forms of comprehensive systems for training of health care workers. Secondly, the bulk of the elderly population will still be concentrated in high density areas. Concurrently, other related services, such as Office of Aging ombudsman, who can advocate for respective owners will be more accessible, as will other related services. Transportation and access to media related resources will certainly be more available.

On the other hand, elements like pollution, noise and unsafe situations may be more commonplace, as will higher food and respite care assistant costs. (See Box 17.)

ECONOMIC IMPLICATIONS

The gap in per capita income between non-metropolitan and metropolitan people is widening. According to the Select Committee on Children, Youth, and Families, families in non-metropolitan areas

BOX 17

ECONOMIC FACTORS WHICH INFLUENCE URBAN PROGRESS FOR THE ELDERLY

— General inflation and especially inflation in health care costs.

— An increasing number of persons receiving services.

— Expanding (and expensive) technology

— Increase utiliution of expanding services.

OTHER POPULATION FINDINGS

— Non-metropolitan persons age 65 years of age and older formed 13 percent of the total non-metropolitan population while the elderly in general constituted 11.3 percent of the nation's population in 1980.

— The highest concentrations of elderly people are in rural villages of 1,000-2,499 population (15.4 percent) and small towns of 2,500-10,000 (14.7 percent). The lowest concentrations are in urban fringe areas (10 percent) and central cities (12 percent).

— Over 500 non-metropolitan counties far exceed the national average in the proportion of elderly, with one-sixth or more of their populations 65 years of age or more. They are concentrated in mostly agricultural areas of the Midwest from which many young people have moved, and in growing retirement areas of Texas, the Ozarks, Arizona and Florida.

— Nearly 500 non-metropolitan counties had high net immigration of people age 60 or more from 1970 to 1980. Between 1975 and 1980, more than a quarter million people of this age moved to non-metropolitan areas (Taeuber, 1983; Smith, Willis and Weber, 1987).

are hard hit by the country's changing economy: "While median family income dropped by only one percent between 1979 and 1986 in urban areas, family income plummeted ten percent in rural communities." Waning income in rural areas results, in part, from long-term agricultural declines. Other rural residents, however, face similar problems.

Fallout from adjustments to the declining rural economy is also clearly evident in an array of personal and family problems in rural U.S. households. Analysis of the rural economic crisis suggests that an increased rate of social, psychological, and emotional problems strikes both farm producers and other residents of declining rural communities (Glasgow, 1988).[26]

Farm vitality is closely associated with rural economic opportunities. Changes in agricultural technology and markets have forced many farm families to devise new strategies to compete and survive on farms.[27]

Service industries now employ more workers than manufacturing, and more jobs have been created in services than were lost in manufacturing and resource-based industries (Smith, Willis and Weber, 1987). The allocation of on- and off-farm work, the linkage between household incomes, and the community's economy are central to the survival and success of rural families. Judging from such patterns of rural employment, rural America as a whole is undergoing fundamental adjustments that promise to alter, forever, rural life in the United States.

By the end of this century, more than two-thirds of the U.S. labor force may be employed in information, knowledge, and service/education jobs. Less than one-fourth may be employed directly in manufacturing and agriculture. Successful performance of the former jobs will require use of computers and advanced telecommunication linkages. Because of the trend towards smaller work organizations and the independence of many of these jobs from a particular locale, it may be possible for rural America to compete for them.[28]

POPULATION SHIFTS

According to Taeuber (1983), "the older population is growing faster than the rest of the population and will be an increasing proportion of the U.S. population over the next 50 years. . . ." However, older Americans are not now and will never be a homogeneous group subject to sweeping generalization. Improvements in income and longevity, for example, that have taken place over the last two decades have made the earlier years of retirement much better today than in 1960. But the situation is quite different for the very old.

Florida has the largest proportion of residents aged 65-plus. In fact, the proportion of elderly in Florida — 17.7 percent — is close to the proportion expected nationally in the year 2020. Florida is also the nation's oldest state, with a median age of 36.0 in 1986 as compared with the youngest state, Utah, with a median age of 25.5.

Houston, Texas, was the major metropolitan area with the smallest percentage of elderly in 1980, with less than seven percent. In absolute numbers, only the New York metropolitan area had over one million elderly residents at the time of the 1980 census.

In 1980, for the first time, a greater number of 65-plus persons lived in the suburbs than in the central cities. The growth of the suburban elderly population has touched every major region of the United States. According to results of a nationwide sample of 2,300 suburbs, the average suburban population in 1980 was 11.8 percent elderly. For the first time, in 1980, a greater number of older persons lived in the suburbs (10.1 million) than in central cities (8.1 million). Older persons are found disproportionately in suburbs which were established before World War II. These older suburbs also have lower average resident income levels, more rental housing, lower home values, and higher population densities.

Other parts of the country — such as the Sunbelt states — are also experiencing an aging of their population due to the migration of older persons during their early retirement years.

Between 1980 and 1986, the increase in the elderly population continued to be more rapid in the South and West. Although the growth rates for the elderly population in the Northeast and Midwest regions were generally less than the national average, the under-65 populations in many of these states are growing at much slower rates or even declining, resulting in relatively high concentrations of older people in these regions.

Older persons who move to another state are relatively affluent, well-educated, and are frequently accompanied by their spouses. Many older persons who move to nonmetropolitan areas are motivated by positive images of rural or small town life or negative views of metropolitan life. Most have existing ties to the new area, such as family, friends, or property (U.S. Senate Special Committee, 1987-88).

PARTICULAR NEEDS OF THE FRAIL ELDERLY

This group of frail elderly has both a lower average income and a much greater need for health services and living assistance than do younger age groups or elderly in metropolitan areas. However, rural elderly are substantially poorer than the metropolitan elderly population. The non-metropolitan elderly's profile of the poverty rate was 21 percent in 1980 versus 13 percent for metro elderly, while median incomes were $4,111 versus $5,003.[29]

Lower personal incomes of the elderly are explained more by characteristics such as low educational attainment, low occupational status, and not working, than by place of residence. Living without relatives or alone was the major factor contributing to poverty. Further, a fundamental population change is also reflected in the composition of income for the elderly and in particular for non-metropolitan individuals, where access to transfer payments has increased from 7.7 to 13.8 percent in the last 20 years (Smith, Willis & Weber, 1987). According to U.S. Senate Special Committee on Aging (1987-88), the elderly depends more heavily on Social Security for their income than they do on any other source.[30]

According to Meyers (1987) the elderly population as a whole are more likely to require health care assistance of all types, including residential or foster care. The continual aging of the population will create even greater demand for care in the future. Updated health care, paraprofessionals, or trained volunteers can provide a network that allows frail elderly to maintain independence longer. Pressure for the development of small business residential homes comes from many sources. For one, the number of elderly with no family will continue to increase, in part because parents in the 1930's had few children. This will mean more demand for such provisions as foster care of the elderly, halfway houses and cooperatives for the elderly.

MIGRATION AND COUNTERMIGRATION IN RETIREMENT

There is also recent evidence of a new trend called "countermigration" in which a small number of older people, who move to another state at retirement, are moving back home or to a state where family members live. Though this trend is relatively small in absolute numbers, it is statistically significant.

Findings from the Retirement Migration Project show that Florida lost significant numbers of elderly migrants to states outside the Sunbelt—namely Michigan, New York, Ohio, and Pennsylvania, all states which also send migrants to Florida. For example, 56 percent of the more than 9,000 elderly Florida residents who moved from New York between 1975 and 1980 and were born in New York. The average age of these countermigrants was 73 years. For contrast this was more than double the number who moved to New York from Florida between 1965 and 1970. Another Sunbelt state, California, also lost older migrants to other areas—but not to states which generally lose large numbers to California. Those leaving the Sunbelt are more likely to have incomes below the poverty line, and many are disabled or are living in institutions or homes for the aged (The Retirement Migration Project, 1984).

It is not possible to determine whether population growth causes economic growth or vice versa, but they are mutually reinforcing processes. The continued growth of retirement communities suggests that for amenity reasons (e.g., material comfort, higher real estate values and general improved quality of life) elderly migrants have continued to flow into the non-metropolitan sector.[31]

Immigration of older persons can be a positive factor in economic development. Older migrants typically bring pension and/or transfer system income with them, and they save and invest more than younger people, thus increasing the pool of capital available for local investment. Moreover, an increase in the number of older residents typically generates new demand for goods and services for the local economy and public sector. This need increases the demand for labor, which can reduce the local unemployment rate and attract labor-force-age migrants to the community. So while elderly immigration is not without direct and indirect costs, it can provide a basis for economic growth for some.[32]

Of additional interest is the fact that while non-metropolitan counties experienced a significant decline in average annual growth rate during 1980-86, the one area that did increase was characterized as "retirement" (Brown, 1988). Only in the rural counties that specialized in retirement communities, tourism, or government activities was the percentage increase in service jobs greater than in metropolitan areas (Batie, 1988).

Taken together, these data indicate that since 1980 rural economies which have depended heavily on the production of goods (e.g., farm products) have had difficulty retaining their population and/or attracting migrants. Most important, however, is that only service-based non-metropolitan economies, characterized as retirement immigration counties, have grown faster than the national average. In fact, this group of counties accounted for almost two-thirds of all non-metropolitan population growth in 1980-86.[33]

CALL FOR SMALL BUSINESS
RESIDENTIAL CARE HOMES

Smith, Willis and Weber (1987) suggest that having elderly choose residential homes for retirement produces added pressures as well as added opportunities for local decision makers. Not the least important of these pressures is the requirement to supply care services for the elderly, especially to those 85 years of age and above.

A study conducted by Sekscenski (1987) found that dramatically fewer people age 85 and above are discharged from nursing homes in communities with fewer individuals (i.e., 1,000 to 10,000) than for areas of populations of 100,000 and above. Perhaps more small businesses designed to service the elderly could provide more personal or home related care so that confinement in nursing homes for the elderly would not be necessary in all cases.

The challenge for economic revitalization projects is to put considerable information, education, and resources to work on critical issues that maintain family viability. Residential home private businesses can be one way to help revitalize families. A home business such as the one promoted in this handbook could provide an alternative source of income (USDA, 1987).

EXPANDED INCOME OPPORTUNITIES

For many who want to work but have special needs to stay at home, owning a business and operating from home go hand in hand. By 1990, 11.4% of the workforce will be at home with 90% of homeworkers either entrepreneurs or working on a contractual basis. Many people decide to work at home because they have greater flexibility, earn more money, can see more of their families, and can be their own bosses. Because a vast majority of new jobs will be in the service industry, entrepreneurs will rush to that sector (Research and News Update, 1988). The concept of the residential home business is a reflection of this trend. It is both a service business and one which allows the owner(s) to work from a home base (Consumer Sciences Newsletter, 1988). (See Box 18.)

Almost 90 percent of the farm operator families have more income from off-farm sources than from farming. Thus, the current structure of the farm family is heavily dependent on non-farm employment opportunities (Batie, 1988). And, for urban families and the state of the national economy, the need for additive income is just as severe. (See Box 19.)[34]

The current state of knowledge with respect to the importance of income, employment and population change is not clearly definitive. There is no prescription for how to develop both urban and rural areas so that both jobs and economic well-being are enhanced. However, many options are available, and these—combined with rural conditions of economic climate, market opportunities and/or resources—can correlate with successful development. For success, the constancy of change puts high priority on flexibility, experimentation analysis. As well, on creating a process to identify potential, financing adaptation, or growth strategies that would otherwise not be financed and developing needed worker and entrepreneurial skills (Batie, 1988).

Income supplementation and diversification opportunities are essential to ease the adjustments needed when traditional income sources become uncertain or disappear (USDA, 1988).

BOX 18

FEDERAL, STATE, AND LOCAL PARTNERSHIPS

Federal and state assistance can help families diversify and improve its economy if government initiatives are more tightly targeted to areas and people in need, if programs complement the values of independence and self-determination and, if, in the long run, the programs do not counter the incentives of the marketplace. Yet, government assistance will only succeed if local communities develop their own human resources and economic adjustment strategies, as well (Batie, 1988).

Successful local economic development efforts, pro-growth attitudes, and well-organized partnerships of local leaders who work for economic growth are valuable resources for growth (Batie, 1988).

BOX 19

STRATEGIES FOR EXPANDING INCOME OPPORTUNITIES

Investigate the economics cost/benefit of home/family-based businesses and/or diversification.

Investigate family interaction and satisfaction in households that are involved in home-based businesses.

Identify markets for potential "in home" or family-based business enterprises.

Chapter 6

Resources

Some of your best resources will be located by networking with others who own residential care or adult foster care businesses. Sometimes this can be done through state or area associations. Likely your state will have an organization. However, the national organization can be contacted at: 71 E. Main, Tilton, New Hampshire 03276. Phone number is 1-800-456-5035.

Because long-term care systems or referrals have only recently received broad attention, your state may not yet have a respective state association. If this is the case, you might consider organizing one. Through a professional organization, a respite care system could be established as well as a recruitment/referral system for identifying and locating clients. The second most helpful resource will be the state Office on Aging. This resource can provide you with numerous and varied resources. The ombudsman can advocate for you and establish other valuable networking contacts in all areas of working with the elderly.[35]

Check your telephone directory for local information for other helpful organizations such as the following:

- Food and Drug Administration (consumer office)
- American Heart Association
- American Dietetic Association
- American Cancer Society
- USDA Extension Service (this office will have training resources on care for the elderly, for food preparation and nutrition programs).
- Association for Residential Care Operators
- Foundation for Hospice and Home Care

- National Home Care Council
- U.S. Small Business Administration

To aid you further in the assessment of your interest in and capability for starting a small residential home business, several brief rural, suburban and urban case situations of how individuals "got into" or are "currently managing" their businesses are described (Boxes 20, 21, 22, and 23). These may assist you in seeing yourself as a residential owner of a residential care home.[36]

BOX 20

CASE SITUATION #1:
A CURRENT OWNER IN A SEMI-RURAL AREA

This residential home was founded on traditional family principles. These not only shape the lives of the family but also the way the home is operated. Family members felt the need for a care facility that would function like a family: be small enough to offer quality personal care and meet the emotional needs of the elderly. There needed to be an alternative to the impersonal, institutional life as seen in the big care centers. We offer a continuity of care and consistency in staffing that allow for a stabilizing emotional effect.

In our situation I, as a registered nurse, and my mother-in-law, as an occupational therapist, share the responsibilities of running the home. I have an aunt who comes in on Sunday mornings to relieve us so we can attend church, but other than this time we operate without outside help.

BOX 20 (continued)

Our physical plan is a regular home modified only slightly to meet the state's regulatory guidelines. It is a two level 4,000 square foot home, with our residents and one caretaker couple (mother and father-in-law) occupying the first level. On this level there are five bedrooms and three bathrooms, a large family-dining room, a kitchen, and a laundry room. We are licensed for eight residents. The upper level is our own private quarters, here my husband and I and two children reside. This allows us to maintain our privacy which is necessary to our mental health and well-being. We have an acre and a half with a large yard and fruit trees, and also a big garden. Our residents enjoy spending time out of doors, walking, helping in the garden, watching the children play--even participating.

The elderly clients are like extended family members and serve very important roles within the home environment. Just as all the members once had contributions to their own families, so now they do so to ours. There is a closeness, a bond, a working towards the same goal: the chance to show the world that the elderly should not be cast aside and forgotten.

In my opinion, when an elderly person must leave his or her home, there is no better type of environment than this residential home to preserve or restore dignity and give life meaning again.

BOX 21

CASE SITUATION #2:
HOW I BECAME A RESIDENTIAL CARE HOME OWNER:

(The Story of a Rural Family)

As the husband and father in our family, my job required extensive travel and being away from home. Added to this, our two sons decided they wanted to stay in the area to go to school. Consequently, I needed to find another source of income and thus began to explore care business alternatives.

My wife had been involved in a personalized care business where she helped recently widowed individuals solve personal/Financial situations. Plus, my wife's mother was well known in the area and was the type of community member who seemed to attract people who had no place to go and help them. For example, she'd help them find places to stay, give them temporary nurturing and/or basic financial assistance.

BOX 21 (continued)

As some of the people with whom my wife worked became older, two asked if they could come live with us. Consequently, we started out with two older residents.

Since I was ready for a change and our family needed a different housing situation, our family made the decision to build facilities that would accommodate a residential home business. Both my wife and I believed this would be an appropriate alternative. She had five fine years experience in her small in-home business and I had experience in helping to care for my grandparents--also for five years.

I also took EMP (Emergency Medical Preparedness) training and this greatly facilitated communication with the medical profession. It also provided an additional competence. Concurrently, I asked a number of doctors if they would be willing to refer elderly who needed or were interested in residential home services. Several doctors assured me they could refer enough patients on their own to fill my facility. After extensive research and interviews with appropriate state offices, we applied for licensing.

When we started, we wanted to manage only eight elderly clients, but almost immediately we went to twelve. The number you serve is determined by personal objectives of the owner/operator. For around six, two people (often husband and wife) can manage without outside help except the need for occasional respite care. If there is a need to hire regular outside help, then you can contract easily with 12 to 16 residents.

Our business is bonded by philosophies of quality service and getting back to the "basics of family living"—to treat people like they would like to be treated. This includes providing choices, thereby allowing each individual to remain as autonomous as possible.

Our facilities were designed with great care and concern for safety, comfort, and enjoyment. For example, windows are low to the ground to allow easy access or escape if necessary. The fact that the elderly can see out of doors, enjoy nature and the landscape, as well as watch weather patterns, improves the quality of their day-to-day experiences. We also emphasize quality food service because mealtime is very important. Good nutrition is required, but beyond this, good cooking of favorite dishes is vital. As owners, we do not merely meet all the basic standards but also go beyond them in our style of individual care. We maintain a sense of humor and demonstrate extensive amounts of patience.

BOX 22

CASE SITUATION #3:
A CURRENT OWNER IN A SUBURBAN/URBAN SETTING

My husband and I had four children who were raised in the house where we currently live. The house is two floors with a large family room, an office, work room and garage on the first floor. The kitchen, large L shaped living dining area and four bedrooms and two baths are on the second floor. The laundry is off the kitchen. Our home is located in a suburban neighborhood that has most services (bus, church) available nearby.

The children were married or in school and I was working in a local church organized child care/adult care center as the office manager. My husband worked as a city supervisor.

My mother had been living in Texas near my sister, but when she suffered a stroke and could no longer live alone, the family bad to make a decision about "who would care for mother." My sister was not married but had total responsibility for her children, who were still at home.

Because of my management background and experience with the church care center, I knew quite a bit about what is required of a respective care worker. Plus, my mother had financial means to pay for assistants. Based on these facts, my husband supported me in the decision to start a business catering to only three upper-income women, one of whom was my mother.

Our home is very comfortable and large enough to afford our clients privacy. We also made the decision to provide more support such as trips to the doctor because our upper-income clients could afford to pay for the "extras."

The process of caring for three elderly women is a very enjoyable task. With my management skills, I feel that I am very responsible and accountable. My records are very well maintained and up to date. In fact, I believe my residential care home is a model.

By catering to women who are more likely to engage in quiet activities, daily life concentrates more on reading, relaxing on the deck off the kitchen when weather permits, feeding the birds, resting and enjoying T.V. more than anything else. They help in the kitchen with some tasks such as setting the table, cleaning vegetables, baking, etc.

BOX 23

CARE SITUATION #4:
AN EXAMPLE OF AN URBAN MINORITY RESIDENTIAL CARE OWNER SITUATION

I am 55 years old and have lived in an inner city Black area all my life. I have a daughter who is 32--with two children who formally got off welfare by taking a LPN (nurses aid) training course. I also have two grandsons who live in the area but who do not work.

My uncle, who was a veteran, died about five years ago and left me $10,000. I realized all around me I had a number of relatives and friends who were growing a lot older and had no one to help them. Most of my people are on Medicade.

In my neighborhood there are a lot of old buildings and run down housing areas. I decided to rent what used to be an old hotel/boarding house and try to go into business for myself. I figured my adult children could help me. I had helped them a lot in the past and they needed something to do anyway.

I decided on this place because it had a big open living room area, with nice big windows and places for plants. My kids and I painted and cleaned and I bought some basic furniture at house sales and used furniture places. It's also close to a neighborhood clinic and a bus line.

I like to cook and have always cooked for a large family.

I don't think I could have succeeded without my church support. They helped me line up people who needed a place. The neighborhood advisor, also at the church, helped me decide on rates and charge and policies to set up. They also helped me establish credit for food supplies until the money started coming in.

I really like to do this kind of work and I feel proud to be able to care for others. There are a lot of family members around that I can call on to help and my eight elders like to have more people around.

The disadvantage is that some of the bedrooms are on the second floor but we made a bedroom there for one on my sons. He sleeps on the second floor and helps the folks to get up and down the stairs.

I don't mind if I work all the time because I never went any place anyway.

Chapter 7

Summary
and Conclusions

Knowledge must be produced before it can be extended. The research and program development base required establishing residential care homes needs to be developed further if quality of life standards are to be promoted for elderly people. This handbook represents "knowledge" that can be applied to meet these needs (Turner and Helena, 1987).

The initiative of creating small businesses to support the development of family income from opportunities that I have proposed is clearly within the scope of many people. These efforts help redefine the approach of research toward the issues of the economy, families, and communities. By stimulating participations from community development persons, social scientists, and economists in many disciplines and arenas, this type of program initiative could add to the critical efforts addressing contemporary economic and family issues.

One thing is clear about the future (see Box 24), the major economic health care issue will not be whether—in the face of other public expenditure problems, such as urban flight, national defense, and pollution—we can have better services for the aged but rather it will be "how we face the long-term health care issue" (Schutz, 1988). As residential home care owners, we can be in a strategic position to promote the growth of resident care as a means to improve the quality of life for those frail elderly who can no longer live alone (Williams, 1990; Williams, 1991).

BOX 24

THE FUTURE

What about the future? We need revolutionary change to rescue the elderly and family in need. We can find answers to questions and must do so without delay by devoting to these problems the same kind of talent, ability, study, and research that have been given to social problems in the past. This challenge for services cannot be avoided.

NOTES

1. Life within a "family" that cares is still the one remaining haven for social support for all human beings.

2. The function of residential homes is to provide "family style care" for elderly who are fundamentally in a positive state of health, but who, for a variety of reasons, can no longer remain independent. These elderly do not need nursing (medical) care; rather, they respond better to a social, family care model.

3. If you find information in this text to be of interest, your first task should be to contact your state Department of Public Welfare or Health and Human Services to obtain copies of respective standards and requirements.

4. Residential homes help the elderly remain in the community where they want to be, and increases their ability to socialize, that is, to participate in family-like affairs. This, in turn, enhances their mental and social well-being.

5. These data verify the innovative opportunity that exists throughout the United States for entrepreneurial activities related to private, for-profit residential care for the elderly.

6. The point is that with both the length of stay and rate of discharge from short-term hospital care, elderly will likely need other available alternatives, such as residential homes.

7. An added benefit of residential home care is health monitoring and early detection of disease. The continuity of residential care — have one person who has close personal contact with the elderly individual — makes it possible to detect depression or other illnesses in early stages. Thus, the success of treatment will likely increase.

8. In the residential home environment, personal attention can encourage the interests, skills, and hobbies of the elderly which also increases the qualities of their lives.

9. Trained health para-professionals, health care entrepreneurs, and/or volunteers can provide a network that allows the frail elderly to maintain a quality life style, including as much independence as possible.

10. Show and give affection to the elderly. Talk to them. Just because they are advanced in age, their emotional needs have not

disappeared. The elderly are hungry for affection and clearly need opportunity to recall special events and good times in their lives. Let them hold hands, have partners, show affection. Always reinforce good behavior.

11. There are constant changes in the federal health care delivery system — particularly in the area of long-term care. Continue to check with your state regulatory office.

12. People routinely turn to members of their social network for help and information before contacting professionals to seek help; Individuals' social networks vary widely in size; size alone is not the crucial variable in determining whether a network is positive or negative; personal skill in activating a positive network can be increased; personal interpretation of a network mediates negative impacts; if a depressed person has a negative interpretation of her/his network, this is associated with low impact on the network; the evidence suggests that a mixture of kin-based networks and other types of network is best for preventing abuse and neglect.

13. Our emotional lives are as important — perhaps more so — than our financial lives. A balance between the two can give our lives more stability.

14. Working at home has taken on new meaning for more than 10 million Americans. The drive for economic self-sufficiency has motivated large numbers of persons to market their skills and talents for profit from home.

15. The more you can have in written agreements, the less conflict can occur. All agreements can be revised as needed. Simply date each revision.

16. Home health care workers may be registered nurses, physical therapists, or personal-care providers who assist with grooming or dressing. These individuals are sometimes homemaker-home health aids. Increasing service-oriented economy offers a widening spectrum of opportunities for customized and personalized small business growth.

17. One family explained it's way of obtaining respite care: the four owners (mother, father, son, and daughter-in-law) rotate "times away."

18. As time goes on, you may wish to develop other forms, such as fire drill directions, etc.

19. Should you feel that your accounting knowledge is so rudimentary that you need professional assistance, the classified section of the local newspaper or the yellow pages of the telephone directory can lead you to a number of accounting services. Many of them are home-based entrepreneurs themselves and know what you will be going through.

20. Money is the lifeblood of any business, so keeping track of the flow coming into and going out of your business is essential to survival, growth, and profit. But the truth is, many business people see record keeping as a necessary evil and devote as little time to it as possible. In fact, record keeping can be a positive experience when it provides you with information about the business that is accurate, organized, and up to date.

21. Some believe these are unnecessary. A more complete system uses the business checkbook plus a cash receipt journal and a cash disbursements journal. However, you may wish to consult the Rowe and Bently (1987) Financial Record Keeping resource.

22. There are a number of balance sheet form variations. You may wish to ask your banker for the form that your bank uses for small businesses — especially if you expect to ask for a loan or use services from that bank.

23. Many farm families remain on the farm because one or more members generate earnings from non-farm activities.

24. Family income can be generated by entrepreneurial development of home-based businesses.

25. More than 19 million persons reported some type of work at non-farm homes last year, and an increasing number of home-workers are farmers. Greater numbers of men (55 percent) than women (45 percent) reported this type of work, but women worked more hours per week (11 hours/women; 9 hours/men).

26. Traditionally, the immediate family has been the primary "caretaker" of its elderly family members. However, with the increase of women who work outside the home and with the fact that adult children typically move away from parents, the "caretaker" systems will change dramatically in the future.

27. Since the late 1960's, 83 percent of the job growth in rural areas has been in services; this trend accelerated in the 1970's.

28. The development of skilled community leadership in rural

areas enhances the ability of local residents to work together. Knowledge about opportunities can be increased; research, implementation, and evaluation can be ensured and aimed at: (a) forming new business, (b) capturing existing income possibilities, and (c) using available aids. Sustaining a decentralized rural population requires a viable infrastructure of transportation, health care, education, and housing.

29. Growth of the elderly population in small towns and rural areas has been about 2.5 percent annually in recent years (Beale, 1982).

30. "Between 1966 and 1984, the U.S. transfer payments grew at an average annual rate of 7.10 percent" (Smith, Willis and Weber, 1987).

31. "Communities that attract retirees, and that incorporate their transfer monies into the community economic base, implicitly exercise a strategy of local development and investigation that fosters greater stability . . . and as well, growth" (Smith, Willis and Weber, 1987).

32. These demographics strongly stress the need for residential home services to be available to rural elderly and, further, that residential home businesses can be one of the basics in rural-economic growth.

33. According to Brown (1988), other variables which greatly influenced jobs and services were local urbanization, location with respect to urban transportation networks, general economic activities, such as employment, the level of well-being, climate, and geographic location.

34. According to Honadle (1987), National Program Leader for Economic Development, Extension Service, USDA, the nature and distribution of America's population is changing and the rural American population is aging as young people migrate to the cities in search of economic opportunities. As people are displaced from farming, there is increasing need to provide alternative jobs. The goal is to increase jobs, means, and government revenues while producing a high quality of life in the community.

35. Developmental (social, physical, intellectual) information on the "frail elderly" can be obtained from your local Cooperative Extension Home Economists or Office on Aging.

36. If you are still interested and feel the need to seek extra training and support, consult a skilled team of business advisors such as accountants, bankers, and attorneys. Your area Office on Aging may also offer some assistance.

REFERENCES

AARP, (1985). *Eating For Your Health*. 1909 K. Street N.W., Washington, DC 20049.

AARP, (1987). *A Handbook About Care in the Home*. A Publication of Health Advisory Services Program Department. 1909 K. Street N.W., Washington, DC 20049.

AARP, (1987). *Nursing Home Life: A Guide For Families*. A Publication of Health Advisory Services Program Department, 1909 K. Street N.W., Washington, DC 20049.

AARP, (1988). *A Profile of Older Americans*. 1909 K. Street N.W., Washington, DC 20049.

AARP, (1988). *Health Insurance News*. 5, (1), Winter. The Prudential Insurance Company.

American Council of Life Insurance Company Services. (1989). *Selecting Long Term Care Services*. 1001 Pennsylvania Avenue N.W., Washington, DC 20004-2599.

Ashley, J. C. And Arnold, D. R., (1986). *Feasibility Checklist for Starting a Small Business*. U. S. Small Business Administrator, Office of Business Development, Management Aids Number 2.026.

Batie, S.S., (1988). Rural Economic Development: Opportunities and Obstacles. *National Rural Studies Committee Proceedings*. Hood River, Oregon, May 24-25, 1988.

Beale, C.L., (1982). *Rural Older Americans: Unanswered Questions*. U.S. Congress, Senate Special Committee on Aging. Hearing, 97th Congress, 2nd Session, May, 19. Washington, DC, U.S. Government Printing Office.

Bennion, M., (1980). *Introductory Foods*. New York: Macmillan Publishing Co., Inc. Seventh Edition.

Brown, D.L., (1988). *Beyond the Rural Populations Turnaround: Implications for Rural Economic Development*. National Rural

Studies committee Proceedings, Hood River, Oregon, May 24-25.

Eliason, C. (1988). *The Business Plan for Homebased Business*. U.S. Small Business Administrator, Office of Business Development, Management Aids Number 2.028.

Glasgow, N., (1988). *The Non-metropolitan Elderly: Economic and Demographic Status*. USDA Economic Research Service, Rural Development Research Report #70, Superintendent of Documents, U. S. Government Office, Washington, DC 20402 (Stock number 001-019-00570-0).

Gunn, B., (1988). Housing for an Aging Society: How Relevant is Age? *Housing and Society*. *15*, (3).

Hall, D., (1988). Help For the Caregiver. *AARP Health Insurance News*. *5*, (4), Fall.

Halpert, B. and Isbell, L. (1988). *Adult Day Care: A Home Economics Guide*, University of Missouri, Columbia Extension Division, College of Home Economics.

Home Call of Oregon. (1987). *Helping To Make Home the Place To Be*. A licensed home health service. 2238 Loyd Center, Portland, OR 97232.

Honadle, B.W., (1987). *Statements from the National Program Leader for Economic Development Extension Services*. USDA Subcommittee on Energy and Agriculture of the Committee in Small Business. U.S. House of Representatives. October 22.

Isabell, L. and Halpert, B. (1986). *Adult Day Care*. Louisiana Cooperative Extension Service, Louisiana State University Agriculture Center.

Internal Revenue Service, Publications Dept. Rancho Cordova, CA. Hot line #1-800-829-3676.

Jones, P. (Ed), (1988). *Aging*. U.S. Department of Health and Human Services, Office of OHDS. Administration on Aging. #358.

Lambell, R. et al., (1988). *Agriculture and Rural Viability*. Experimentation Station Committee on Organization and Policy. Cooperative State Research Service. North Carolina State University, Chapel Hill, N.C.

MacLeon, H., (1987). *Caring For Your Parents, a Sourcebook of*

Options and Solutions for Both Generations. Garden City, NY: Doubleday and Company, Inc.

Merrick, J., (1985). "Health Insurance Forum." *Eating For Your Health.* A Guide to Food For Healthy Diets., AARP, 1909 K Street N.W., Washington, DC, 20049.

Meyers, S.S., (1987). Economic Status of Elderly is a More Severe Problem in Non-Metropolitan Areas, *Sociology of Rural Life.* Minnesota Extension Service, University of Minnesota, *9*, (3), Fall.

Price, B.A., (1982). *Datatrack* Social Research Services, American Council of Life Insurance, 1850 K Street N.W., Washington, DC 20006.

Research and News Update, *(1988). Consumer Services Newsletter*, Texas Agriculture Extension Service, *4*, (1), January.

Rogers, D., (1986). *The Adult Years.* An Introduction to Aging. 3rd edition. NJ: Prentice-Hall 07632.

Rowe, B.R. and Bently, M. T. (1987). *Getting Started: A Home Based Business Workshop*, Volumes: Getting Started; Developing Your Business Plan; Setting a Price; Financial Recordkeeping; Managing Your Financial Assets; Mapping Your Marketing Strategy; Acquiring Capital; Working With People; Keeping Track of Taxes; Selling Your Product; Copyrights, Patents, and Trademarks. Cooperative Extension Service, Utah State University, Logan, Utah, 84322-3505.

SBA, *Directory of Business Development Publications.* #115A (8-88) U.S. Small Business Administration, Office of Business Development, Mail Code 7110. Washingtion, DC 20416.

Schmall, V.L. et al., (1988). *Families and Aging*, A Guide To Legal Concerns, Extension Circular, 1221 Oregon State University Extension Service, Corvallis, Oregon, July.

Segal, S.P. and Moyles, E.W., (1988). Residential Care: A topology of Residential Facilities. *Adult Foster Care Journal. 2*, (2). Summer.

Sekscenski, E.S., (1987). Discharges From Nursing Homes: Preliminary Data from the 1985 National Nursing Home Survey. NCHS (National Center for Health Statistics) *Advance Data*, #142. September 30.

Sirocco, A., (1988). Nursing and Related Care Homes as reported from the 1986 Inventory of Long-Term Care Places. NCHS. (National Center For Health Studies) *Advance Data*, #147. January 22.

Smith, G.W., Willis, D.B., and Weber, B.A., (1987). The Aging Population, Retirement Income and the Local Community. *Community Economics* WRDC #36. July. Western Rural Development Center, Oregon State University, Corvallis, Oregon 97331.

Summary 1987: National Hospital Discharge Survey, NCHS (National Center for Health Statistics). *1988 Advance Data, 159*, September 9.

Taeuber, C.M., (1983). America in Transition: An Aging Society. *Current Population Reports, Special Studies.* Series R-23, #128, U.S. Dept. of Commerce, Bureau of the Census.

Turner, J.S. and Helena, D.B., (1987). *Lifespan Development.* 3rd edition. New York: Holt, Rinehart and Winston.

USDA, (1985). *Dietary Guidelines for Americans.* U.S. Department of Agriculture and U.S. Department of Health and Human Services. Food and Drug Administration, 5600 Fishers Lane, Rockville, Maryland 20857.

USDA, (1987). *Revitalizing Rural America.* Cooperative Extension National Initiatives. ESUSDA, Washington, DC.

USDA, (1988). *Eight National Priority Initiatives.* Cooperative Extension National Initiatives. ESUSDA, Washington, DC.

Schutz, J.H., (1988). *The Economics of Aging.* 4th edition. Massachusetts: Auburn House Publishing Co.

The Retirement Migration Project. (1984). The Center For Social Research in Aging, the University of Maine, September.

U.S. Senate Special Committee on Aging. (1987-88). *Aging America: Trends and Projections.* U.S. Dept. of Health and Human Services. LR 3377(188). D 12198.

Williams, D.K., (1990). Small Business Opportunities in Residential Care Services for Rural Elderly Persons. *Adult Residential Care Journal. 4*, (1).

Williams, D.K., (1991). The Quality of Life for Elders in Residential Care Environments. *Adult Residential Care Journal. 5*, (3).

For Product Safety Concerns and Information please contact our EU representative GPSR@taylorandfrancis.com Taylor & Francis Verlag GmbH, Kaufingerstraße 24, 80331 München, Germany

T - #0151 - 270225 - C0 - 212/152/7 - PB - 9780789000668 - Gloss Lamination